Classic Cars

Classic Cars

RICHARD GUNN

amber
BOOKS

This edition published in 2019
Copyright © 2003 Amber Books Ltd

Published by
Amber Books Ltd
United House
North Road
London N7 9DP
United Kingdom
www.amberbooks.co.uk
Instagram: amberbooksltd
Facebook: www.facebook.com/amberbooks
Twitter: @amberbooks

ISBN: 978-1-78274-916-5

Project Editor: Michael Spilling
Design: Zoe Mellors

Printed in China

Picture Credits: International Masters Publishing BV

Contents

Introduction   6

INTRODUCTION

In 1885, a middle-aged German engineer named Karl Benz built a small carriage. Nothing too unusual in that perhaps, but Benz's three-wheeled contraption was a little different. Instead of a horse, it used a primitive four-stroke petrol engine for motive power. The era of the motor car had arrived, and Karl Benz was the man responsible for ushering it in.

Benz did not just invent the automobile though. He changed the world. His 1885 tricycle may have been basic in the extreme, with its 0.75 kW (1 bhp) single-cylinder engine capable of just 16 km/h (10 mph), but this was the start of both a revolution – one which gave unprecedented personal freedom to millions.

The car has come a long way in the hundred or so years since its birth, changing beyond all recognition from the simplistic, spluttering devices of the Victorian era. Today's horseless carriage is a technological wonder. Even the most humble family run-around is more efficient, more reliable and more technologically advanced than most of the best offerings of

Ford's Model T brought motoring within the reach of the masses. Later, it became a popular hot-rod choice.

just a couple of decades ago. And an average car now has more computing power than that used in the Apollo moon landings.

Looks too have been transformed. The first automobiles genuinely did look like carriages without the horses attached, built by traditional coachbuilders still trying to adapt to new ideas. Over a century, the car has gradually evolved its own shape, becoming longer, sleeker, more aerodynamic and more visually appealing as it became less about getting from A to B and more about displaying the status of its owner.

So, today's cars are better than ever, more capable at their job than the pioneering engineers of yesteryear could ever have dreamed of. So why is there still such an interest in classic cars? Why do millions of motoring enthusiasts worldwide still choose to restore and drive cars which are now technologically obsolete?

The answer lies in nostalgia. Cars may have improved, but they have done so at the loss of their character and individuality. Once upon a time, vehicles were designed by just a few people, experts in their field who injected their creations with passion and inspiration, even a soul. Now they're put together on a computer, worked on by a committee and then costed by men in suits to see if they're financially feasible. Styling has become less varied and interesting as a result. In the past, it was easy to tell a Ford from a Fiat, a Chevrolet from a Cadillac, a Volkswagen from a Volvo. Now you can only tell from the badge.

Government safety and emissions regulations, which first started to really bite in the 1970s, have become rampant. The proliferation of personal transport has brought major problems throughout the world. Roads are congested, driving is no longer the pleasure it used to be and the motorist is fast becoming a vilified member of society, blamed for all manner of environmental and social evils.

No wonder then that people look back to a golden age of motoring, before big business and governments got too involved with motoring. It may be a case of looking back with rose-tinted spectacles, but driving once seemed so much more fun and cars so much more glamorous, stylish and exciting. It's these kind of iconic classic cars which are celebrated by this book.

Defining the breed

But what exactly is a classic car? It's not an easy thing to pin down. Some regard classics as any kind of working car from the late 1970s and before. There's a general acceptance now that any car over 20 years old is a classic.

Others will cite past vehicles built by the premier marques – Rolls-Royce, Ferrari, Aston Martin, Cadillac and the like – as the only true classics, dismissing anything more mainstream and affordable as simply old rusting wrecks.

Many will define a classic as just a superb, distinctive car of any age; after all, surely a sporting Jaguar or Dodge Viper is worthy of modern classic status from the moment it leaves the factory? And there are more still who bestow classic standing just on looks alone. Cars like the Jaguar E-type, Bentley R-type Continental, Porsche 356 or Buick Riviera are still some of the most beautiful creations of recent times, almost mobile sculptures, technical art exhibits on wheels. Looks are often more prized than performance; it's that initial visual impact that always counts the most. Love at first sight is a reality with many classics.

Last, but by no means least, there are those pioneering vehicles which introduced new concepts or advancements into the motoring world, like the Chrysler Airflow which boldly featured streamlining before the market of the 1930s was quite ready to accept it, or more recently and very differently, the Saab 99, which blazed the way for turbocharging on modern, affordable, family cars. Not all were successful, some – like the Airflow – were complete disasters. But they're all regarded as classics for simply trying something different.

The truth is that nobody has ever come up with a final, all-encompassing definition of a classic car, and probably never will. It embodies all the above descriptions, and more besides. The term is refreshingly vague, embracing all manner of vehicles from rusting wrecks up to stunning supercars. Few would argue that a Volkswagen Beetle isn't worthy of the classic accolade, but so too is a brand new Aston Martin Vanquish, one of the most glorious British-built cars for years. On the surface, the two have little in common,

one a humble mass-built sedan, the other a fabulously expensive sports car strictly for the rich. Yet both are classics.

Perhaps the best explanation of a classic car is that it is any vehicle, of any age and in any condition, admired by somebody. Different people find different things to appreciate in a car. For some, it's the sheer power of a vehicle, for others it's all about styling and appearance. Some esteem luxury and splendour, while others celebrate the

The 1959 series Cadillac personified the flamboyant 'fins and chrome' era.

Britain once led the world in sports cars, with the Austin-Healey 3000 a well-loved example.

the Ferrari Dino, Lamborghini Miura and Rolls-Royce Silver Cloud are celebrated because they are the pinnacles of the motoring world, the breeds by which others of their type are judged. Cars which have become famous across the globe due to their appealing qualities and longevity – like the Mini, the Citroen 2CV and the Fiat 500 – are featured. Then there are the motoring curios, like the Amphicar – a failed attempt to build an amphibious car for the masses – and the Edsel, which went just a little too far with its 1950s styling excesses and became motoring's largest financial flop.

Most eras are covered. Inevitably, the majority of the cars come from the 1950s,

failures of the auto world, those oddball vehicles which tried to pioneer new features, or were simply so incompetent at what they did that they earned a good-natured following just because of it.

This book is an appreciation of this diversity and there's an eclectic mix of cars within these pages. It includes the good, the bad and, in some cases, the downright ugly, from all over the world. True greats, such as

1960s and 1970s, the golden period when car ownership took off, and some utterly incredible machines were produced. But this book stretches back to the turn of the 20th century, with the Ford Model T, one of the best-selling and best-known cars of all time, responsible for introducing both mass-production and the concept of affordable motoring for all. It also encompasses cars which are still in production, like the Subaru Impreza and Dodge Viper, all examples of cars which are unparalleled in their class.

Inevitably, not everybody will agree with the choices. Out of the countless thousands of cars which have now earned classic status (by whatever means), this book features just 75, so there are some notable omissions in all categories. Benz's original 1885 horseless carriage, the classic which started it all, would have been an surefire inclusion in a bigger book. There are many American cars which made the shortlist but which didn't quite make it, such as the Tucker Torpedo,

Chevrolet Bel Air and Plymouth Fury to name but a few. And almost every Ferrari, Bentley or Lamborghini ever built could have been covered without too many raised eyebrows, but again, there's no space for them all. Hopefully though, this book stands as a representative selection of some of the best and most intriguing classics around.

The classic car movement

Enthusiasm for classic cars has never been more intense than it is now. But it was only in the 1970s that interest in post-war cars started to grow, both in America and Europe. Motoring enthusiasts on both sides of the Atlantic started to pay attention to the rapidly disappearing ranks of old vehicles, both the humble and the exceptional.

Older cars had a lot going for them. There were plenty around, they were cheap to buy and easy to work on, yet still usable on the road. By choosing an older vehicle, owners made a statement about themselves, that they were not prepared to accept the increasing blandness of modern cars, and weren't concerned about having to own the latest model just to keep up with everybody else around them.

Gradually, the movement grew, slowly at first, but gathering more momentum as owners clubs, specialists and suppliers were established to support what were now regarded as historic vehicles.

The lure of classic cars had reached such levels by the mid-1980s that the hobby began to attract unwelcome attention from those more interested in money than preservation and restoration. Classics started to be exported around the world to make a quick buck and prices sky-rocketed. Even the values of everyday classics, whatever their condition, shot up, while thoroughbred marques wearing prestigious badges reached ludicrous levels.

It couldn't last. The bottom was bound to drop out of the artificially inflated market at some point, and it happened at the end of the 1980s when a global recession hit and prices fell rapidly. It was an ironic touch that the cash-hungry investors who got their fingers burned so badly during the classic car boom had been responsible for saving some classics that would otherwise have been scrapped. The real enthusiasts would never have been able to afford it.

In recent years though, there has been interest in classic cars from another unexpected quarter. Searching for ways to sell more cars, modern manufacturers have looked towards their past for design cues. Retro-styling is suddenly all the rage. Ford has recently built updated versions of its original Thunderbird and GT40, while the look of the Chrysler PT Cruiser owes much to the hot rods of the 1940s. Volkswagen has rebuilt its Beetle for a new generation, and the new MINI, albeit built by BMW, has carried over much of the character of the original. Car firms have began to

Modern it may be, but the Dodge Viper's looks and performance have endowed it with instant classic status.

and do their utmost to keep them on the road. There will always be the greats of yesteryear, and future classics will emerge to join their ranks. Years from now, classic car fans will be enthusing about the current Beetle and MINI models the way the afficionados of today take delight in the originals.

In the meantime, this book is a commemoration and a history of some of the most exhilarating, exciting and evocative vehicles from the last 100 years of motoring. Above all, it celebrates classic cars, their inestimable magic, and the joy they have brought to millions of enthusiasts. Enjoy both the cars, and this book.

realize that heritage sells. Many companies maintain their own classic car fleets, either for publicity purposes, or simply out of a need to occasionally revel in past glories. Others – like BMW and Volvo – have even started manufacturing parts for their older vehicles again.

It all adds up to an unprecedented level of interest in classic cars, and a worldwide movement which has never been healthier. Whatever happens to motoring in the future though, classic cars will always be around, as will the enthusiasts who appreciate them

AC Cobra

Take an attractive British roadster, and squeeze in a variety of American V8 engines. That is just what Carroll Shelby did to create the legendary Cobra.

Cobras came as open two-seaters only. Luxury and comfort was not an option, but there was a removable soft-top for those moments when the weather just got too much...

Ford supplied the engines for the AC Cobras. The 4,736 cc (289 ci) small block V8 engine was the first to make an appearance, but in 1965 came the Cobra 427, with its massive 6,997 cc (427 ci) engine, enough to make it the fastest-accelerating production car around.

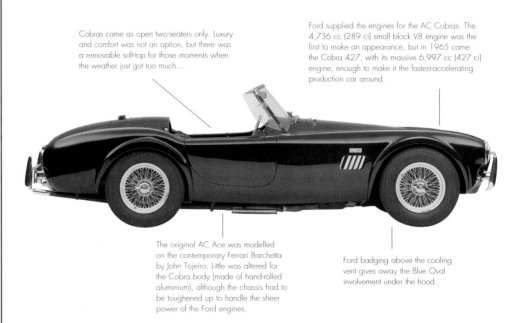

The original AC Ace was modelled on the contemporary Ferrari Barchetta by John Tojeiro. Little was altered for the Cobra body (made of hand-rolled aluminium), although the chassis had to be toughened up to handle the sheer power of the Ford engines.

Ford badging above the cooling vent gives away the Blue Oval involvement under the hood.

There was little frontal protection
in the event of any small accident.
The bumpers – what there were of
them – were just chromed tubes.

Performance was so
awesome that disc brakes
were a necessary fitting.

Side exhausts were an option usually
found on racing models, increasing
both power and noise levels.

UNITED KINGDOM/UNITED STATES

There are few things to top an AC Cobra for sheer, brutal power and shattering performance. The Cobra was a demon on the road, a wild beast few drivers were capable of taming properly. Everything about the car was ferocious, it was almost the equivalent of just sitting astride a powerful V8 engine and hoping you could hold on.

The Cobra started life as the British AC Ace, in 1953, fitted with a six-cylinder engine dating back almost to World War I. Then, in 1961, AC was approached by Texan racing driver Carroll Shelby,

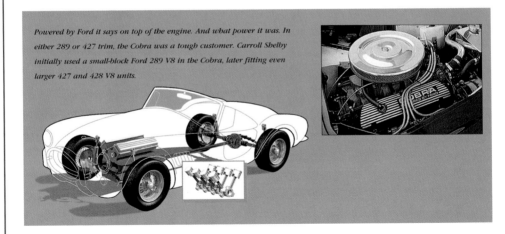

Powered by Ford it says on top of the engine. And what power it was. In either 289 or 427 trim, the Cobra was a tough customer. Carroll Shelby initially used a small-block Ford 289 V8 in the Cobra, later fitting even larger 427 and 428 V8 units.

who suggested the Ace would be much improved with a V8 engine fitted. The legend of the Cobra had begun.

British Aces to American Cobras

Production started in 1962, with chassis and bodies being shipped to California for Shelby to work his magic with the engines and other American components. After the first 75 cars were built using big Ford 4,260 cc (260 ci) V8 engines, manufacture was standardized on the 4,736 cc (289 ci) V8.

When it came to racing, Cobras were practically unbeatable, and Shelby took the World GT Championship in 1964 using specially bodied coupés.

But Shelby wanted more. Much more! In 1965, he created the Cobra 427, using the monster Ford 6,997 cc (427 ci) V8. With that in place, nothing could out-accelerate a Cobra, 0 to 96 km/h (60 mph) coming in just over four heart-stopping seconds.

Flared arches and wide tyres signified that the new snake meant real business.

The iconic Cobra slithered to a stop in 1968, although the chassis lived on in the new AC428 coupé. Its place as one of the most potent racers ever was assured.

AC Cobra

Top speed:	225 km/h (140 mph)
0-96 km/h (0-60 mph):	5.5 secs
Engine type:	V8
Displacement:	4,736 cc (289 ci)
Max power:	202 kW (271 bhp) @ 5,750 rpm
Max torque:	386 Nm (285 lb ft) @ 4,500 rpm
Weight:	918 kg (2,020 lb)
Economy:	5.3 km/l (15 mpg)
Transmission:	Four-speed close ratio manual
Brakes:	Four-wheel discs
Body/chassis:	Separate chassis with two-door body in aluminium

ALFA ROMEO SPIDER

The charming Alfa Romeo Spider stayed in production for an extraordinary 27 years, a testament to its timeless styling and long-lived appeal in a competitive marketplace.

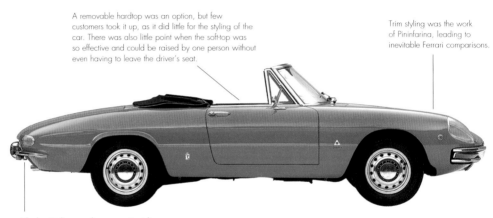

A removable hardtop was an option, but few customers took it up, as it did little for the styling of the car. There was also little point when the soft-top was so effective and could be raised by one person without even having to leave the driver's seat.

Trim styling was the work of Pininfarina, leading to inevitable Ferrari comparisons.

The boat-tail rear end was a pretty styling touch, lasting until 1970, when it was replaced by a Kamm tail.

Like the Jaguar E-type, the Spider was forced to lose its faired-in headlamps for the US market due to American lighting rules.

The traditional Alfa Romeo grille was displayed proudly on the nose, although big bumpers on the later cars would compromise its appearance.

The original bumpers – if they can be called that – may have looked stylish, but they were of no use even in the slightest knock. Bigger ones would be fitted later, especially for American versions, where Federal regulations would require bulky impact-resistant bumpers to be adopted. The 1983 to 1986 Aerodinamica had body-moulded bumpers.

ITALY

The Spider name debuted on an open top Alfa Romeo model – the Giulietta – in 1955. But it was the range of cars introduced in 1966 that held the title for the longest, bearing the Spider name through to 1993. A production run of 27 years for any model is a considerable achievement, but in the fiercely competitive sports car sector, it verges on the astounding.

Pininfarina's pretty boat-tailed roadster wasn't called the Spider initially. Alfa Romeo received 140,000 entries when it

This is the light alloy 1750 twin-cam engine, used in the Spider from 1967 to 1971. It is regarded as one of the greatest four-cylinder Alfa Romeo engines, and for the US, was fitted with Spica mechanical fuel injection. Bore and stroke is 80 mm (3.15 in) by 88.39 mm (3.48 in).

held a competition to name its new car. Suggestions like Lollobrigida, Bardot and the bizarre Stalin were rejected in favour of the Duetto. And it was this model which Dustin Hoffman drove to stardom in *The Graduate*.

The Spider name reappeared in 1967, when the larger 1,779 cc (109 ci) engine was fitted to the car, officially becoming the 1750 Spider Veloce. With its (troublesome) Spica mechanical fuel injection and five-speed transmission, it was pointed firmly at the American market. The smaller-engined 1300 Spider Junior joined it for 1968.

Changes for a new decade

Some of the original purity was lost in 1970 when the sleek boat-tail rear was lost in favour of a squared-off Kamm end, and further 'updates' throughout the decade robbed the Spider of much of its looks, although it always remained an attractive, dashing sports car. The engine had been enhanced in 1971, with the introduction of a 1,962 cc (118 ci) unit, although it did little to improve top speed.

1993 finally saw the end of one of Alfa Romeo's most attractive, delightful and memorable models ever, its longevity and looks earning it true classic status.

Alfa Romeo Spider

Top speed:	190 km/h (118 mph)
0-96 km/h (0-60 mph):	10 secs
Engine type:	In-line four
Displacement:	1,779 cc (109 ci)
Max power:	101 kW (135 bhp) @ 5,500 rpm
Max torque:	186 Nm (137 lb ft) @ 2,900 rpm
Weight:	1,052 kg (2,315 lb)
Economy:	9.9 km/l (28 mpg)
Transmission:	Five-speed manual
Brakes:	Four-wheel discs
Body/chassis:	Steel monocoque with two-door convertible body

ITALY

AMPHICAR

When it comes to weird vehicles, they do not come much stranger than the Amphicar – the swimming machine that gave a completely new meaning to off-roading.

Rear fins were the highest on any production car, even a 1959 Cadillac, but weren't just for show. They were necessary to help water

As well as road lights, Amphicars were also fitted with boat navigation lamps, necessary to comply with Coast Guard regulations.

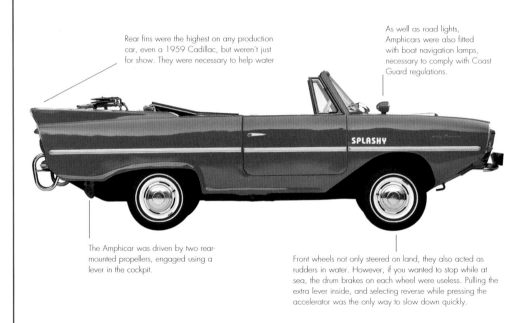

SPLASHY

The Amphicar was driven by two rear-mounted propellers, engaged using a lever in the cockpit.

Front wheels not only steered on land, they also acted as rudders in water. However, if you wanted to stop while at sea, the drum brakes on each wheel were useless. Pulling the extra lever inside, and selecting reverse while pressing the accelerator was the only way to slow down quickly.

Optional extras for the Amphicar included an anchor, floating cushions, flares, cleats and an all-important paddle in case of breakdown!

Despite its compact proportions, the Amphicar was a full four-seater, complete with folding roof for rainy weather or rough seas.

The trunk held the same engine as used in the British Triumph Herald sedan, although with extra waterproofing used. The hood was the place to keep any luggage.

GERMANY

23

The bizarre Amphicar was an attempt by German engineer Hans Trippel to build an affordable amphibious vehicle that would sell 20,000 vehicles a year. Such ideals were inevitably doomed to failure, but Trippel's surreal vision of combining car and boat nevertheless resulted in one of the world's most fascinating automobiles.

Trippel had been building amphibious machines since 1935, but when the Quandt family, owners of BMW, showed interest, his dream of producing a mainstream production vehicle seemed set to come

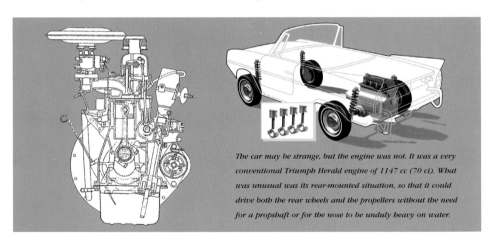

The car may be strange, but the engine was not. It was a very conventional Triumph Herald engine of 1147 cc (70 ci). What was unusual was its rear-mounted situation, so that it could drive both the rear wheels and the propellers without the need for a propshaft or for the nose to be unduly heavy on water.

true. Five million dollars were pumped into the project and, in 1962, the first Amphicars made their debut.

They were a curious mixture of different parts. The body was Italian, the transmission was Porsche, and the brakes were Mercedes. The rear-mounted 1,147 cc (70 ci) engine and electrics came from the British Triumph company. Top speed on land was, allegedly, 105 km/h (65 mph), and 11 km/h (7 mph) on water. The use of mild steel kept production costs down, but created potentially disastrous problems when corrosion started to appear and leaks followed soon afterwards.

A sinking feeling

Right from the start, the Amphicar failed to stimulate the level of interest it needed to survive. Between 1962 and 1968, around 4,500 were sold, just over a quarter of the projected annual production. Most went to the United States.

Despite some epic sea voyages from Africa to Spain, San Diego to Catalina Island, and England to France in a gale, ultimately the Amphicar was just too much of a compromise to be taken seriously.

Amphicar

Top speed:	105 km/h (65 mph)
0-96 km/h (0-60 mph):	43 secs
Engine type:	In-line four
Displacement:	1,147 cc (70 ci)
Max power:	32 kW (43 bhp) @ 4,750 rpm
Max torque:	83 Nm (61 lb ft) @ 3,200 rpm
Weight:	1,050 kg (2,312 lb)
Economy:	12.4 km/l (35 mpg)
Transmission:	Four-speed manual
Brakes:	Four-wheel drums, plus anchor
Body/chassis:	Unitary monocoque construction with steel two-door convertible body

GERMANY

ASTON MARTIN DB5

Driven by James Bond, desired by everybody else, the DB5 was the definitive British grand tourer that made Aston Martin world-famous during the 1960s.

Non-standard modifications on 007's DB5 included an ejector seat, tyre slasher, rear bullet shield, radar tracker, revolving numberplates, hydraulic rams, oil jets, smokescreen and machine guns behind the sidelights.

Side vents were a well-known Aston Martin feature, still found on current DB7 and Vanquish models.

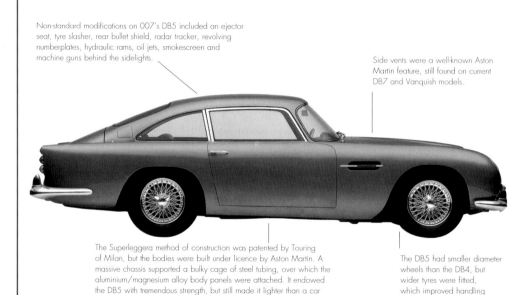

The Superleggera method of construction was patented by Touring of Milan, but the bodies were built under licence by Aston Martin. A massive chassis supported a bulky cage of steel tubing, over which the aluminium/magnesium alloy body panels were attached. It endowed the DB5 with tremendous strength, but still made it lighter than a car with a conventional steel body.

The DB5 had smaller diameter wheels than the DB4, but wider tyres were fitted, which improved handling at high speed.

The easiest way to tell a DB5 from its DB4 predecessor is by reference to the headlamps. The DB5 has faired-in light units, although the DB4GTs and the last DB4 Vantages also had this styling feature.

The DB5 featured Girling disc brakes, a big improvement over the Dunlop items previously used.

A ston Martin's DB5 can lay claim to being the most famous car ever. Why? Because in 1964, James Bond (007) drove one in *Goldfinger* and, suddenly, it seemed everybody in the world wanted to own a DB5. However, it would only be a very privileged few who could afford to buy and run this superbly suave British grand tourer.

The DB5 wasn't so much new as a gradual evolution of the previous DB4. Introduced in summer 1963, it retained the DB4's Superleggera construction (an

Aston Martin engineer Tadek Marek was responsible for the all-alloy six-cylinder engine, which was the mainstay of the Aston range from the DB4 until well into the 1970s. It featured twin overhead camshafts with seven main bearings, and came with three SU carburettors as standard.

aluminium body clothing a steel skeleton), but incorporated 170 modifications. Most notable were the cowled front headlamps, lending the car a purposeful, more streamlined look, even if they did slightly compromise high-speed driving at night.

The Vantage advantage

Under that stylish body was an enlarged version of Aston Martin's potent six-cylinder alloy engine with twin camshafts. Engineer Tadek Marek expanded it to 3,995 cc (244 ci), and three SU carburettors gave it 210 kW (282 bhp). In 1963, a Vantage version was introduced, with triple Weber carburettors pumping up the power to a ferocious 234 kW (314 bhp).

Most DB5s emerged from Aston Martin's Feltham and Newport Pagnell factories as sedans, but the car could also be bought as a very handsome drophead coupé, or as a shooting brake estate car. Only 12 were of the latter were made, making them extremely desirable today.

Just over 1000 cars were built in total, before the DB5 was superseded by the more aerodynamic, but heavier, DB6 in 1965.

Aston Martin DB5

Top speed:	230 km/h (143 mph)
0-96 km/h (0-60 mph):	8.6 secs
Engine type:	In-line six
Displacement:	3,995 cc (244 ci)
Max power:	210 kW (282 bhp) @ 5,550 rpm
Max torque:	379 Nm (280 lb ft) @ 4,500 rpm
Weight:	1,568 kg (3,450 lb)
Economy:	5.3 km/l (15 mpg)
Transmission:	Five-speed manual
Brakes:	Four-wheel discs
Body/chassis:	Steel platform chassis with steel tube body frame and aluminium two-door coupe body

UNITED KINGDOM

ASTON MARTIN DBS V8

The DBS was a new Aston for a new era. It was a large, muscular beast, with styling that would continue for 23 years.

The shape wasn't as sleek as the previous DB6 and the extra weight of the four-seater Aston meant that it was slower than the car it was intended to supersede. It was only when the V8 engine was introduced that the DBS got the extra power it both needed and deserved.

The DBS first appeared with the same six-cylinder engine as the DB6. It was always designed for V8 power though, and finally got it in 1969.

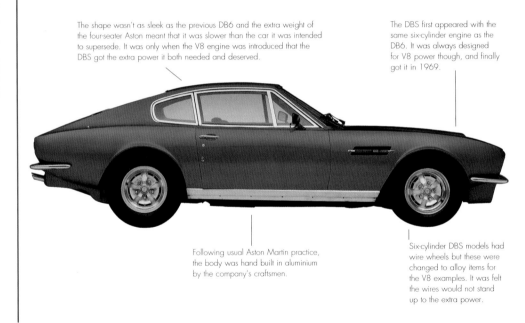

Following usual Aston Martin practice, the body was hand built in aluminium by the company's craftsmen.

Six-cylinder DBS models had wire wheels but these were changed to alloy items for the V8 examples. It was felt the wires would not stand up to the extra power.

William Towns was responsible for the styling. He'd started work at Aston Martin as a seat designer, and the DBS was his first car for the company. American influences were very apparent in his design.

In 1972, when the car was renamed as just the V8, the front was restyled with a different grille and single headlamps.

As stylish and popular as the DB models were, by the late 1960s, they were starting to age. The design dated back to the late 1950s, and Aston Martin felt it needed a replacement for the 1970s. Enter, in 1967, the big Aston Martin DBS, styled by young designer William Towns. The new car was bulkier and heavier, and was based on a lengthened and widened DB6 chassis to accommodate four occupants. It still used

The DBS's original six-cylinder engine was soon changed for a new V8 with twin overhead camshafts for each bank of cylinders. Aston Martin engineering legend Tadek Marek designed the more powerful all-alloy unit, which would have powered the DBS right from its birth, if only it had been ready in time!

aluminium bodywork, but dispensed with the Superleggera construction process (see DB5 entry).

The new Aston Martin flagship had always been intended for the company's new V8 engine, designed by Tadek Marek, but the engine wasn't ready in time. Thus, many critics found the DBS underpowered. Their objections were silenced when the all-aluminium twin overhead camshaft V8 appeared at last in 1969, creating the DBS V8.

Unfortunately for Aston Martin, the 1970s were a decade of financial instability. First, owner David Brown sold the firm in 1972, and the new custodians redesigned the front of the car, calling it just the Aston Martin V8. But problems for the firm and the car continued. In 1975, just 19 were sold.

Vantage model

Despite everything, the company persevered. In 1977, the awesomely powerful Vantage, with uprated engine appeared, earning a reputation as one of the fastest production cars in the world. The next logical progression was a convertible, which followed in 1978. The V8 car (but not the engine) was finally dropped in 1990.

Aston Martin DBS V8

Top speed:	257 km/h (160 mph)
0-96 km/h (0-60 mph):	5.9 secs
Engine type:	V8
Displacement:	5,340 cc (326 ci)
Max power:	239 kW (320 bhp) @ 5,000 rpm
Max torque:	488 Nm (360 lb ft) @ 4,000 rpm
Weight:	1,727 kg (3,800 lb)
Economy:	4.3 km/l (12 mpg)
Transmission:	Five-speed manual
Brakes:	Four-wheel vented discs
Body/chassis:	Unitary monocoque construction with aluminium and steel two-door coupé body

UNITED KINGDOM

33

ASTON MARTIN LAGONDA V8

It looked like a concept car, yet the razor-edged Lagonda saloon of 1976, with its futuristic and controversial styling, stayed in production for 14 years.

Designer Williams Towns started work at Aston Martin designing seats but then went on to style the DBS of 1967. The Lagonda was his most outlandish design for the company though, intended to make a startling visual impact, an exercise in mobile flamboyance. The 1987 Series 2 restyle introduced rounder lines.

The engine came from the Aston Martin V8 sedan, but was detuned slightly to make the Lagonda more manageable.

Most of the car's underpinnings came from the standard Aston Martin V8 sedan, but the floorpan was stretched by 30 cm (1 ft), exactly the length of the glass panel set halfway along the roof.

On the earliest cars, wheel centres were colour-co-ordinated with the body.

An electronic dashboard, with touch sensitive controls, was the most innovative interior feature. But it proved unreliable in service, and bright sunshine made the digital displays difficult to read.

As well as the standard sedan, customers could choose an even longer stretch limo or specify a Tickford bodykit.

The design incorporated a traditional Lagonda grille, although the low lines meant it had to be modelled in miniature.

UNITED KINGDOM

35

As stunning as its cars have been, Aston Martin generally played safe with styling. It knew its customers, and realized anything too much out of the ordinary might damage sales, which were already difficult to come by in the energy-conscious 1970s. All that changed in 1976 when the radical Lagonda V8 sedan appeared on the scene.

The troubled Lagonda firm was bought by David Brown shortly after Aston Martin, in the late 1940s. However, little was done

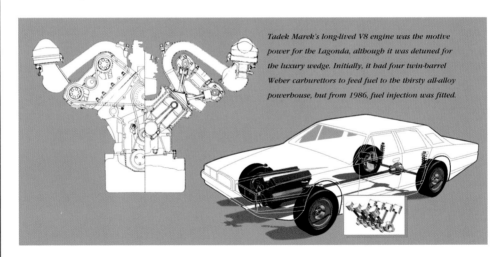

Tadek Marek's long-lived V8 engine was the motive power for the Lagonda, although it was detuned for the luxury wedge. Initially, it had four twin-barrel Weber carburettors to feed fuel to the thirsty all-alloy powerhouse, but from 1986, fuel injection was fitted.

with the marque until after he had sold both companies. In 1976, the new owners revitalized the name with the launch of an extravagant luxury sedan which explored the extremes of styling.

The ultimate wedge

The wedge shape was a popular design idea during the 1970s, but few went as far with the concept as William Towns, responsible for the car's style. Cutting edge had never seemed so sharp.

Beneath the hand-built alloy body was the usual Aston Martin V8 engine and stretched floorpan with softer suspension for a smoother ride. However, the flamboyant exterior was mirrored by the luxury hi-tech interior, sporting ground-breaking digital controls. The electronics were so far ahead of their time that, most of the time, they did not work properly.

But that didn't stop the amazing-looking Lagonda grabbing headlines and sales across the world. 600 cars were built between 1976 and 1990.

The Lagonda was Aston Martin's most outrageous production car, but it was a financial success and helped save the firm.

Aston Martin Lagonda V8

Top speed:	232 km/h (144 mph)
0-96 km/h (0-60mph):	8.8 secs
Engine type:	V8
Displacement:	5,340 cc (326 ci)
Max power:	242 kW (325 bhp) @ 5,600 rpm
Max torque:	508 Nm (375 lb ft) @ 4,500 rpm
Weight:	2,104.5 kg (4,630 lb)
Economy:	4.9 km/l (13.8 mpg)
Transmission:	Chrysler TorqueFlite 727 three-speed automatic
Brakes:	Four-wheel discs
Body/chassis:	Integral chassis with four-door aluminium and steel sedan body

UNITED KINGDOM

AUBURN SPEEDSTER

The advanced styling of the Auburn Speedster was years ahead of its time. With a supercharged engine, it also had the speed to match its sleek looks.

A small hatch behind the cockpit concealed the folded soft-top, helping to add to the Auburn's wind-cheating lines.

Every Auburn Speedster had a plaque on the dashboard confirming it had been driven to over 161 km/h (100 mph) during testing.

The flying lady mascot – reminiscent of Rolls-Royce's Spirit of Ecstasy – was repeated on the sides as well as the hood. The side ones were made by slicing a radiator item in two.

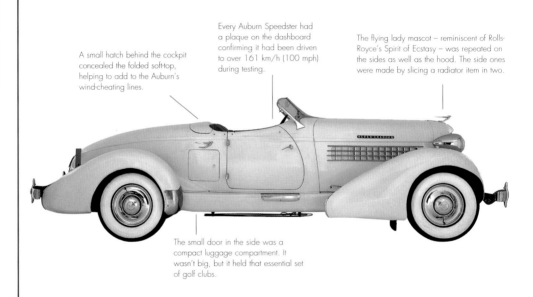

The small door in the side was a compact luggage compartment. It wasn't big, but it held that essential set of golf clubs.

The long, streamlined hood hid the Lycoming straight-eight engine. The mechanically driven supercharger boosted power to 112 kW (150 bhp).

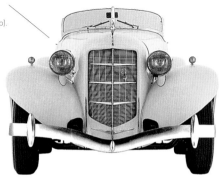

The transmission was novel. It was a three-speed unit but the driver could choose between low and high ratios, effectively giving six gears. In high-ratio top gear, the engine was very relaxed, even at high speeds.

BXY 525

A distinctive feature of the Auburn was its tapered boat-tail rear end, a popular design in the 1920s and 1930s. Gordon Beuhrig, a stylist at Duesenberg (see overleaf), was behind the look.

UNITED STATES

39

UNITED STATES

Prior to the arrival of Errett Lobban Cord in 1924, Auburn had been building mundane cars for middle-class markets. Cord promptly changed all that. He transformed Auburn's remaining stock of vehicles by painting them in glamorous colour schemes and pitching them at younger customers with money to spend and an image to maintain.

In 1928, the Auburns came in for a redesign. The look was more aerodynamic, especially around the rear, where an attractive 'boat tail' was fitted. The engines were simple items, but nevertheless quite powerful.

V12 gamble

When the Depression hit, starting with the Wall Street Crash in 1929, Auburn was

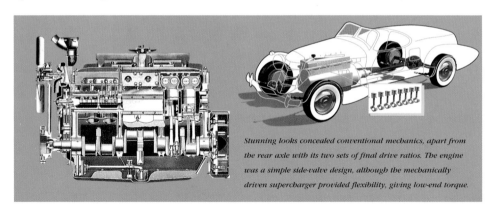

Stunning looks concealed conventional mechanics, apart from the rear axle with its two sets of final drive ratios. The engine was a simple side-valve design, although the mechanically driven supercharger provided flexibility, giving low-end torque.

forced to make cutbacks to survive. The choice was between manufacturing many cheap cars, or a limited range of expensive, classy models. Cord chose the latter option, and the Speedster received a large V12 engine. However, it wasn't a success.

Cord himself moved to England in 1933, amid claims of financial irregularities. Harold Ames of Duesenberg (another Cord company) took over control at Auburn and brought in his own designer, Gordon Beuhrig, to redesign the Speedster.

The 1935 result was an art deco expression of speed and style, using just a revamped rear and curvaceous wings to transform the looks. Supercharging gave the Speedster a top speed of over 161 km/h (100 mph), while the use of two sets of final-drive gears, coupled to a three-speed gearbox, resulted in America's first six-speeder.

These Speedster 851 and 852 models were cheap cars made to look expensive. Unfortunately, although they looked a million

dollars, they couldn't save the company, and Auburn went out of business in 1936.

Auburn Speedster

Top speed:	173 km/h (108 mph)
0-96 km/h (0-60 mph):	10.0 secs
Engine type:	Straight-eight
Displacement:	4,587 cc (280 ci)
Max power:	112 kW (150 bhp) @ 4,000 rpm
Max torque:	Not quoted
Weight:	1,706 kg (3,753 lb)
Economy:	4.4 km/l (12.4 mpg)
Transmission:	Three-speed manual with dual-ratio rear axle
Brakes:	Four-wheel Lockheed drums, hydraulically operated by Bendix vacuum booster
Body/chassis:	Steel two-door, two-seat speedster body with steel box-section ladder-type chassis rails

UNITED STATES

Audi Quattro

One of the best-performing sports coupés of the 1980s, the four-wheel drive Audi Quattro was
revolutionary, a thinly disguised rally car tamed for the road.

Extra features on the Sport
included a rear spoiler and
Porsche 917 disc brakes.

The engine was a five-cylinder unit, initially used
in the Audi 200. It was turbocharged for extra
performance. Audi claimed that the five cylinders
were more economical than six, but gave just as
smooth a performance. In truth, there just wasn't
room to fit in a larger six-cylinder block. The
Quattro's engine could be tuned to produce over
447 kW (600 bhp).

The suspension was identical at both
ends: all-round MacPherson struts, with
lower wishbones. Both the front and
rear are fitted with anti-roll bars.

The four-wheel drive inspiration came from Volkswagen's Iltis military truck. The rear differential came from this vehicle when the Quattro went into production.

This car is a Sport Quattro, built primarily to satisfy rallying regulations which dictated that road-legal production versions had to be built. Its body was a mixture of fibreglass and strong but lightweight Kevlar, built on a shortened wheelbase. The Sport cost three times the price of a standard Quattro.

Yes, there are rear lights. They are just blacked out, a feature introduced in 1984.

Many people regard the Quattro as the definitive car of the 1980s. When it burst onto the motoring scene in 1980, it was a complete shock. There was nothing like it in existence and it set new trends that continue today.

The Quattro was at home in any environment. It could handle any surface, be it asphalt, gravel, mud or snow and could tackle each with equal levels of performance. On roads, it had exemplary speed and handling, yet was also content

The five-cylinder configuration of the Quattro's engine was unusual for the time, and was carried over from the previous Audi 200T. The engine only had an alloy-cylinder head, but for the Sport Quattro, there was an aluminium block too, as well as a bigger turbocharger.

to drive around town as an everyday vehicle. It was a car for all reasons.

Military beginnings

The origins of the Quattro could be found in the military VW Iltis truck, with its novel four-wheel drive system. Instead of a conventional transfer box (heavy, complex and uneconomical), the drive to the rear of the Iltis was by means of a hollow output shaft. Simple, but effective.

In 1977, a prototype Audi 80 sedan was fitted with the Iltis system, and Audi began to realize that it had the beginnings of a world-beating road and rally car on its hands. Further development continued, using as many components from existing Audi and VW models as possible. By March 1980, the car was ready to be unveiled.

Rallying victories followed thick and fast, while the road cars soon picked up a great reputation for usability and reliability. In 1983, a more potent, shortened version of the Quattro, known as the Sport, was launched. It still looked understated, but had an extreme twin-camshaft, 20-valve engine.

Audi pulled out of rallying competition in 1986, but the road Quattro continued to be made until 1991.

Audi Quattro

Top speed:	248 km/h (154 mph)
0-96 km/h (0-60mph):	5.0 secs
Engine type:	In-line five
Displacement:	2,133 cc (130 ci)
Max power:	228 kW (306 bhp) @ 6,700 rpm
Max torque:	350 Nm (258 lb ft) @ 3,700 rpm
Weight:	1,303 kg (2,867 lb)
Economy:	4.6 km/l (13 mpg)
Transmission:	Five-speed manual with drive to all wheels
Brakes:	Four-wheel vented discs
Body/chassis:	Monocoque two-door coupé

GERMANY

AUSTIN-HEALEY 3000

The combination of the Healeys' sports car design and Austin's three-litre engine resulted in a powerful and brutal open two-seater with classic lines.

The simple cast-iron engine was the same as the one used in the stately Austin Westminster sedan. However, it was made more powerful when installed in the Austin-Healey. Final versions of the car were tuned to produce 110 kW (148 bhp).

Low ground clearance caused many problems and resulted in costly exhaust bills for owners. The clearance was improved from 1964, but it was still all too easy to scrape the bottom while driving.

Steel wheels were an unpopular option and most Healeys appeared with wire wheels with centre-lock spinners.

Despite still being a very raw car, the final 3000s were quite civilized compared to earlier Austin-Healey models. The windscreen was wraparound, the side windows were wind-up, and the soft-top was improved. There was even wood veneer on the dash.

Austin-Healeys were capable of high speeds, so fitting servo-assisted front disc brakes on the 3000 was a wise decision by the company.

The traditional Healey grille was a diamond shape but was changed over the years into the oval profile.

The low, sleek looks were helped by the rear axle mounted above the chassis rails.

UNITED KINGDOM

47

S tar of the 1952 London Motor Show was a stylish roadster designed by father-and-son team Donald and Geoffrey Healey. Among its admirers was Leonard Lord, the chief of Austin. As his firm had already supplied the engines and running gear, Lord was closely associated with the car, but when he saw the public appreciation, he decided that Austin should build and market the car as well.

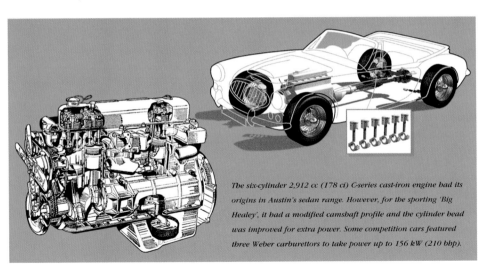

The six-cylinder 2,912 cc (178 ci) C-series cast-iron engine had its origins in Austin's sedan range. However, for the sporting 'Big Healey', it had a modified camshaft profile and the cylinder head was improved for extra power. Some competition cars featured three Weber carburettors to take power up to 156 kW (210 bhp).

This decision led to the creation of a potent new sports car, the Austin-Healey 100. Its main market was seen as the United States, where it would slot neatly in between the higher-priced Jaguar XK120 and the cheaper MG TD.

The Austin-Healey was a sports car in the traditional sense. There were few concessions to luxury and it needed a skilled driver to get the best handling and performance from it. A Healey could easily turn around and bite back if not treated firmly. But it was also a very rewarding car when properly driven, with large amounts of power on tap.

Up to six

In 1956, a six-cylinder engine was fitted and the body revised to create the 100/6. In 1959, engine capacity was increased even more, and the Austin-Healey 3000 was born, available in both two-seater and (cramped) four-seater versions.

It was the 3000 Mk III of 1963 to 1968 that would be the most refined of the Big Healeys (as they were nicknamed), the many improvements making it not only more cultivated, but more powerful too, although the essential character was still kept.

Austin-Healey 3000

Top speed:	195 km/h (121 mph)
0-96 km/h (0-60 mph):	10.1 secs
Engine type:	In-line six
Displacement:	2,912 cc (178 ci)
Max power:	110 kW (148 bhp) @ 5,250 rpm
Max torque:	224 Nm (165 lb ft) @ 3,500 rpm
Weight:	1,158 kg (2,549 lb)
Economy:	5.9 km/l (16.8 mpg)
Transmission:	Four-speed manual with overdrive
Brakes:	Discs at front, drums at rear
Body/chassis:	X-braced ladder-frame chassis with steel 2 + 2 convertible body

UNITED KINGDOM

49

AUSTIN MINI MK I

They say the best things come in small packages. Never was that more true than when applied to the Mini, Europe's important miniature motoring marvel.

Despite its small proportions, the Mini was spacious inside. Four passengers could be carried in comfort, thanks to the space-saving techniques used by Alec Issigonis. The attempts to maximize interior room was also responsible for the Mini's box-like styling. Its predecessor, the Austin A35, was much more curvaceous.

Mini engines were mounted transversely, on top of the gearbox. This front wheel drive arrangement saved space in the cabin, and also did away with a transmission tunnel running through the car. Additionally, it endowed the Mini with wonderful handling.

A curved front grille and exterior door hinges distinguished the Mk I Minis.

Engine, steering and transmission were all mounted together on a front subframe, which helped cut down on vibration.

The A-series engine first appeared in 1951 and powered all Minis.

A wheel in each corner helped improve cornering ability. With no overhanging bodywork front or rear, the Mini was capable of negotiating bends superbly. The 25.4 cm (10 in) wheels were the smallest on any 'proper' car at the time, another space-saving move by designer Alec Issigonis.

When the Mini debuted in 1959, few could have guessed how important it would become on the motoring scene. Designer Alec Issigonis packed it with innovation. The engine was mounted transversely, with the gearbox in the sump and power came through the front wheels. There was an amazing use of space inside the cabin. The Mini seemed larger inside than outside and would become the benchmark for all subsequent small sedan designs.

The versatile British Motor Corporation A-series engine was first used in the Austin A30 of 1951. It went on to power all manner of British vehicles, but the Mini was probably its most famous fitting.

Owners soon came to love the affordable Mini's agility, superb handling (which could embarrass many more expensive cars) and its cheeky personality. Above all else, Minis were fun.

Mini packaging

Launched originally with Austin and Morris badges, more luxurious Wolseley and Riley versions joined the catalogue in 1961, complete with tiny fins and more chrome. In the same year, the sporty Mini Cooper was launched, with a bigger engine and the car started to dominate motorsport. It excelled most of all at rallying, where its road-holding abilities led it to many victories. When the 1,275 cc (78 ci) Mini Cooper S was launched in 1964, few cars could beat it.

In 1964, the rubber cone suspension was replaced by a smoother, Hydrolastic fluid system. In 1965, automatic transmissions also became available to improve the car and bring it up to date.

The Mini was subtly modified in 1967, to make the Mk II, and again in 1969 as the Mk III. The Mini lasted until 2000, a production run of 41 years. Its name is now continued by the bigger BMW MINI.

Austin Mini Mk I

Top speed:	121 km/h (75 mph)
0-96 km/h (0-60 mph):	26.5 secs
Engine type:	In-line four
Displacement:	848 cc (52 ci)
Max power:	27 kW (37 bhp) @ 5,500 rpm
Max torque:	69 Nm (51 lb ft) @ 2,900 rpm
Weight:	609 kg (1,340 lb)
Economy:	14.6 km/l (40 mpg)
Transmission:	Four-speed manual
Brakes:	Four-wheel drums
Body/chassis:	Unitary monocoque construction with subframes and steel two-door sedan body

UNITED KINGDOM

53

BENTLEY R-TYPE CONTINENTAL

Rolls-Royce may have built 'the best cars in the world', but one of its most spectacular vehicles wore a Bentley badge and the R-type Continental name.

The design of the Continental bore more than a slight resemblance to a Pininfarina prototype mounted on a Bentley chassis, which had appeared at the 1948 Paris Salon. Did the Italian styling influence the R-type shape as well?

The engine was the same as standard R-type, but the wind-cheating body of the Continental meant it was over 16 km/h (10 mph) faster. Later cars were fitted with an enlarged engine, which widened the performance gap even further.

The body was hand-built by coachbuilder HJ Mulliner, and developed in a wind tunnel for maximum aerodynamic effect. The tests also resulted in an exotic, beautifully proportioned body with a shapely fastback rear. Panels were made from aluminium to save weight.

It may have been sporting, but the Continental was still packed with luxury inside, including wood dashboard and trim, leather upholstery and deep-pile carpets.

From the outside, the trunk looked small, but could accommodate six specially fitted suitcases.

A curved Bentley radiator shell had a better drag coefficient than the equivalent squarer Rolls-Royce item.

Fins weren't just a fashion statement. They helped the bulky Bentley to remain stable at high speed.

E ven today, the R-type Continental is nothing short of dazzling. Imagine, then, how it must have looked in 1952, in an austere world still recovering from World War II. Yet this radical design appeared from Rolls-Royce, a company more known for quiet tradition than complete revolution.

The beauty was not just skin deep. The combination of an aerodynamic aluminium bodywork and powerful six-cylinder engine resulted in the fastest production four-

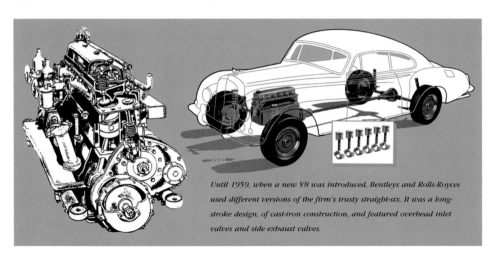

Until 1959, when a new V8 was introduced, Bentleys and Rolls-Royces used different versions of the firm's trusty straight-six. It was a long-stroke design, of cast-iron construction, and featured overhead inlet valves and side exhaust valves.

seater in the world, astonishing for a car that looked like the interior of a stately home inside, and seemed to have similar proportions outside.

Expensive Olga

Such looks, luxury and performance came at a big price though. The R-type Continental also entered the record books as the world's most expensive car in 1952. Over its three-year production run, only 208 cars were built, making this Bentley more exclusive than most.

Go ahead for the Continental had been given in 1950, so the car had an astonishingly short development period. A Bentley Mk VI body was fitted with a prototype body and nicknamed Olga, after its numberplate. Within two years, the car entered production almost unchanged.

The only major alterations to the original concept came in 1954, when the engine size was enlarged to 4,887 cc (298 ci), and

automatic transmission was offered as well as the standard manual gearbox.

The R-type Continental was replaced by the S1 in 1955. However, in 1991, the name was revived.

Bentley R-type Continental

Top speed:	188 km/h (117 mph)
0-96 km/h (0-60 mph):	13.5 secs
Engine type:	In-line six
Displacement:	4,566 cc (279 ci)
Max power:	est 112 kW (150 bhp)
Max torque:	est 199 Nm (147 lb ft)
Weight:	1,611 kg (3,543 lb)
Economy:	5.7 km/l (16 mpg)
Transmission:	Four-speed manual or four-speed automatic
Brakes:	Four-wheel drums
Body/chassis:	Separate chassis with aluminium two-door coupé body

UNITED KINGDOM

BMW 2002 TURBO

Diminutive in stature but a giant in character, the 2002 Turbo was Europe's first turbocharged production car, unexpectedly fast despite suffering from serious turbo lag.

The iron engine block was the same as used in BMW's 746 kW (1,000 bhp) turbocharged Formula One engine, although it was detuned for the 2002 Turbo.

The Turbo retained the 2002 sedan body, but pumped up the muscles. There were flared arches (to accommodate the bigger tyres, which were wrapped around alloy wheels), a front chin spoiler and a rear trunk one, as well. Colourful body graphics completed the 2002 Turbo look.

Turbocharging was still underdeveloped at this time, and the 2002 had a problem with turbo lag. The KKK turbocharger boosted power to 127 kW (170 bhp), but the large rotors were slow to start spinning. The turbo would eventually cut in at around 3,800 rpm.

Taking a cue from emergency vehicles, the 2002 Turbo lettering on the front spoiler was reversed, just in case any drivers looking in their mirror weren't sure what the car rapidly catching up with them was!

To improve handling, the 2002 Turbo had lowered suspension and stiffer springs. It was also given higher ratio steering gear than other 2002 models.

GERMANY

Seventh March 1966 was the 50th anniversary of BMW. The company chose to celebrate in a very special way, launching the first version of the model that would do much to continue BMW's renaissance. The compact 1600-2 model (so named because it had just two doors) formed the basis of BMW's entry level cars well into the latter half of the next decade.

Tests were carried out on fitting a two-litre engine into the 1600-2 bodyshell in 1967, with the subsequent production 2002 model appearing at the start of 1968. Developments followed quickly and within two months,

The Turbo had lower and stiffer suspension compared to the 2002tii on which it was based. The two-litre (121 ci) engine had an alloy head, cast-iron block and KKK turbocharger bolted on. Compared to modern units, the turbocharger was big and lazy, but for the time, it was a real step forward in engine technology.

the 2002ti was announced, featuring twin carburettors. Cabriolet and targa roof versions came at the beginning of the 1970s, joined by the 2002 tii fuel-injected version.

Meanwhile, away from the road, BMW had won four rounds of the 1969 European Touring Car Championship, using a special turbocharged 2002. This success – and continuing strong sales of the 2002 range – convinced the firm to market a turbocharged version for the public. It was a pioneering step for BMW as no other European firm had attempted to build such a car.

Turbo trendsetter

The 1973 2002 Turbo did not just look very different from its less potent siblings. It behaved very differently. It had tighter steering, stiffer suspension and superb performance. Once you got over the initial turbo lag. It set a trend other manufacturers would take years to catch up with. Unfortunately, the Turbo came at completely the wrong time. The oil crisis hit just a few months after the launch of the 2002 and suddenly, fuel-thirsty cars were out of favour. One of BMW's most exciting sedans lasted a scant ten months.

BMW 2002 Turbo

Top speed:	209 km/h (130 mph)
0-96 km/h (0-60 mph):	7.6 secs
Engine type:	In-line four
Displacement:	1,990 cc (121 ci)
Max power:	127 kW (170 bhp) @ 5,800 rpm
Max torque:	240 Nm (177 lb ft) @ 4,500 rpm
Weight:	1,082 kg (2,381 lb)
Economy:	6.4 km/l (18.1 mpg)
Transmission:	Four or five-speed manual
Brakes:	Vented discs, 25.4 cm (10 in) diameter at front; drums, 22.9 cm (9 in) diameter at rear
Body/chassis:	Steel monocoque two-door sedan

GERMANY

61

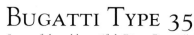

BUGATTI TYPE 35

Successful and beautiful, Ettore Bugatti's Type 35 notched up almost 2000 wins during its heady career, gaining a reputation as one of history's greatest racers.

Type 35s had two seats, one for the driver, the other for the riding mechanic during racing. Little weather protection was provided for either, although at least there was a cowl and fold-down windscreen for the one behind the wheel.

The overhead camshaft 2,262 cc (138 ci) straight-eight engine was complicated for its era. There was no need for a conventional high-pressure oil lubrication system, because the crankshaft ran on roller bearings. 1927's Type 35B had a bigger supercharged engine which put out 97 kW (130 bhp).

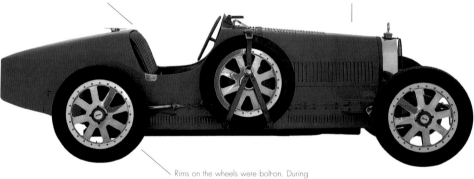

Rims on the wheels were bolt-on. During the 1920s, many racing cars had a potentially lethal problem with punctured tyres separating from their rims at high speeds. The bolt-on Bugatti items were designed to stop this happening.

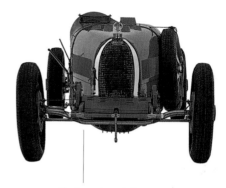

The narrow width of the compact Bugatti meant that the gear lever was situated on the side of the car. It was joined by the handbrake arm too, which was over-long to enable it to be operated more easily.

The front axle was hollow, not only a weight-saving device, but one which enhanced control as well.

FRANCE

63

Italian Ettore Bugatti had been known in auto circles since the turn of the 20th century. He had designed many cars for other manufacturers, but when he found a backer willing to finance him though, he set up a factory in Molsheim, near Strasbourg, and started to build some of the most glorious vintage cars ever crafted, under his own name.

The first of these production cars was the Type 13 of 1910, which set the Bugatti precedents of having an overhead camshaft and a fixed cylinder-head. The engine was four-cylinder though, and it wouldn't be

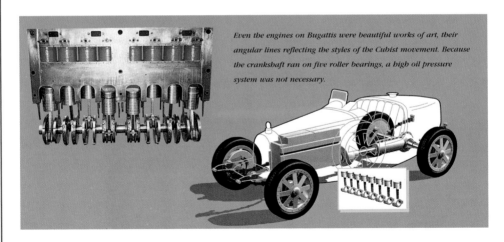

Even the engines on Bugattis were beautiful works of art, their angular lines reflecting the styles of the Cubist movement. Because the crankshaft ran on five roller bearings, a high oil pressure system was not necessary.

until the 1920s that he ventured into making larger engines, with the eight-cylinder Type 30 of 1922.

The Type 30 was a tourer, but the Bugatti masterpiece following hot on its heels had no such pretensions and was a purebred racer. 1924 saw the debut of the Type 35, still regarded by many as one of the most enchanting racing cars ever.

Racing supremo

It took a skilled driver to get the best out of a Type 35, but the ingeniously designed chassis prompted tremendous handling and in the right hands, a Type 35 could take on all-comers. It took a tough driver too: there was little in the way of comfort within the cramped, open cockpit.

Within a year, the superior Bugatti had begun its domination of the Targa Florio road race a year later, it won the World Championship. The Type 35 racing legend was well under way.

Variations on the Type 35 theme included the lower-powered Type 35A of 1925, the supercharged Type 35C of 1926 and the Type 35B a year later, which not only had supercharging, but a bigger engine too.

Bugatti Type 35

Top speed:	201 km/h (125 mph)
0-96 km/h (0-60 mph):	7.0 secs
Engine type:	Supercharged in-line eight
Displacement:	2,262 cc (138 ci)
Max power:	97 kW (130 bhp) @ 5,500 rpm
Max torque:	Not quoted
Weight:	752 kg (1,654 lb)
Economy:	5.2 km/l (14.7 mpg)
Transmission:	Four-speed manual
Brakes:	Four-wheel cable operated drums, front and rear
Body/chassis:	Tapered channel section steel chassis with two-seat alloy body

FRANCE

BUICK RIVIERA

The elegant but restrained Buick Riviera was one of the most successful American attempts at incorporating luxury European style and performance in a mainstream model.

The man behind the razor-edged, understated design was Bill Mitchell, GM's vice-president of styling. The side windows were electrically operated, with the chrome pillars capable of retracting into the body to give a pillarless coupé look.

Two V8 engines were available for the 1963–65 series of Rivieras. The standard 6,571 cc (401 ci) 'Nailhead' unit was shared with other Buicks like the Invicta, Le Sabre and Electra. For more power, a 6,964 cc (425 ci) V8 could be fitted, as found in the Gran Sport version.

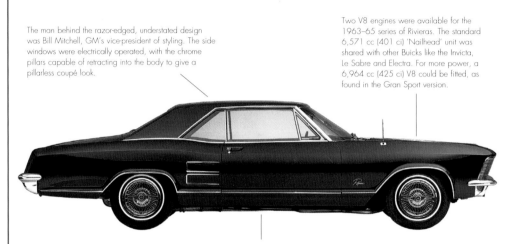

While the Riviera was large by European standards, it was relatively compact by US ideals. It was smaller than other Buicks available at the time and much less imposing than the gargantuan Cadillacs and Lincolns it was pitched against.

The front end, with its simple but dignified eggcrate grille, was inspired by the Ferrari 250 GT. From 1965, the headlamps were stacked in the front bumpers (where the indicators are on this 1963 example) and covered by electrically operated 'clam-shell' doors when not in use.

The exotically named Turbohydramatic automatic transmission was originally two-speed, but went to three-speed for 1965.

The story behind the Buick Riviera is that Bill Mitchell – vice-president of styling at GM – was in London in 1958. He saw a Rolls-Royce glide past and when he returned home, said that GM needed a cross between a Ferrari and a Rolls.

Whether or not it is true, it makes a great myth. It also made a great car. The Buick Riviera would turn out to be the American Bentley Continental, one of the most handsome cars ever created. In an era when big fins and dripping chrome were

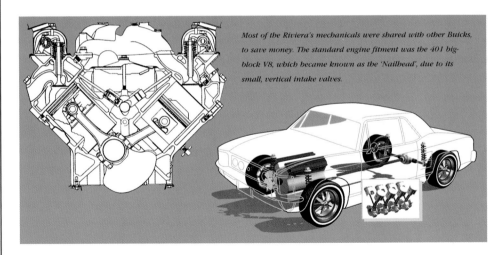

Most of the Riviera's mechanicals were shared with other Buicks, to save money. The standard engine fitment was the 401 big-block V8, which became known as the 'Nailhead', due to its small, vertical intake valves.

still a fad, the 1963 Riviera bucked the trend and set its own style.

The seemingly simplistic lines were deceptive. It was elegantly proportioned, aristocratic to look at and exuded an aura of class few of its rival contenders could match. The sleek front projected a purposeful attitude and the interior was packed with luxury and gadgets. And it was powerful too, fitted with either a 6,571 cc (401 ci) or 6,964 cc (425 ci) V8 capable of taking it to over 201 km/h (125 mph).

Limited edition luxury

Buick helped keep the Riviera exclusive by only building 40,000 a year. A few cosmetic changes were made in 1964, with more major styling revisions following in 1965. Most notably, the headlamps were stacked behind 'clam-shell' covers, which refined the looks even more.

It was all too brief though. For 1966, the old bodyshell was dropped, and the second generation Riviera grew larger, losing much of its original charm as it did. Every passing year saw it become more bloated, although the 1971 to 1973 series had a glorious boat-tail rear end.

Buick Riviera

Top speed:	201 km/h (125 mph)
0-96 km/h (0-60 mph):	8.0 secs
Engine type:	V8
Displacement:	6,571 cc (401 ci)
Max power:	242 kW (325 bhp) @ 4,400 rpm
Max torque:	603 Nm (445 lb ft) @ 2,800 rpm
Weight:	1,985 kg (4,376 lb)
Economy:	4.3 km/l (12 mpg)
Transmission:	Two-speed automatic
Brakes:	Four-wheel drums, 30.5 cm (12 in) diameter
Body/chassis:	Steel body, on separate X-frame chassis

UNITED STATES

1959 Cadillac Series 62/De Ville

The '59 Caddy was the epitome of the flamboyance of 1950s America, a chrome-laden and finned monument to the United States' love affair with the automobile.

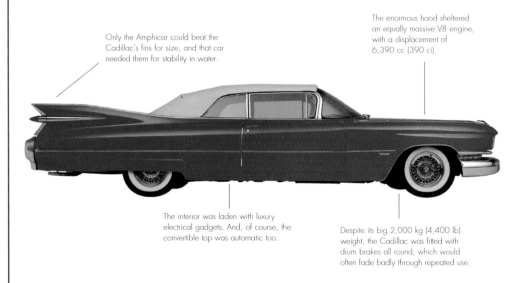

Only the Amphicar could beat the Cadillac's fins for size, and that car needed them for stability in water.

The enormous hood sheltered an equally massive V8 engine, with a displacement of 6,390 cc (390 ci).

The interior was laden with luxury electrical gadgets. And, of course, the convertible top was automatic too.

Despite its big 2,000 kg (4,400 lb) weight, the Cadillac was fitted with drum brakes all round, which would often fade badly through repeated use.

Headlamps would turn on automatically at dusk and also switch from high to low beams for oncoming traffic. Cadillac dubbed them Twilight Sentinels. Such a system would be innovative on a car even today.

Styling – particularly at the rear – was influenced by the American space programme. The car was designed by the legendary Harley Earl. The big chrome pods on either side of the bumpers concealed the reversing lamps.

Eight headlamps at the front? Not quite. The top four are driving lights, those mounted on the bumper are parking lamps.

The '59 Caddy was most at home on big, wide roads. The turning circle was massive, at 7.3 metres (24 ft).

UNITED STATES

UNITED STATES

Britain has Rolls-Royce, America has Cadillac. The two marques have always appealed to similar customers in their respective countries, but in very different ways. While Rolls-Royces have traditionally been understated and dignified, Cadillacs have usually gone to the other extreme, packing in as much extravagance, glamour and glitz as possible on four wheels.

Influenced by the new era of jet and space travel, Cadillacs had first started to sprout

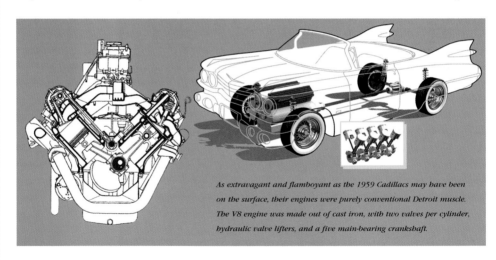

As extravagant and flamboyant as the 1959 Cadillacs may have been on the surface, their engines were purely conventional Detroit muscle. The V8 engine was made out of cast iron, with two valves per cylinder, hydraulic valve lifters, and a five main-bearing crankshaft.

fins in 1949. Under the stylistic direction of Harvey Earl, America's car design guru, Caddy fins gradually grew larger until they reached their zenith in 1959, with the De Ville and Eldorado.

The 1959 Cadillacs seemed to personify the spirit of post-war American optimism. Flashy, brash and over-the-top to foreign eyes less used to such automotive exuberance, the cars were impossible to ignore. They dominated the roads in a way no other vehicle could, looking for all the world like grounded rocket ships on tyres.

Style, not speed

The flamboyant theme was continued inside. Interiors were massive, swallowing six passengers with ease and surrounding them with expansive luxury and electrically operated gadgets. Air suspension provided a soft, floating ride, albeit one with considerable body roll on corners. However, Caddies were for taking it easy, not speeding, despite

their hefty V8 power. Most desirable of all the cars were the convertibles, the ultimate in luxury cruising.

In the view of many enthusiasts, a 1959 series isn't just the definitive Cadillac. It's the definitive American classic car.

1959 Cadillac Series 62/De Ville

Top speed:	195 km/h (121 mph)
0-96 km/h (0-60 mph):	11.0 secs
Engine type:	V8
Displacement:	6,390 cc (390 ci)
Max power:	242 kW (325 bhp) @ 4,800 rpm
Max torque:	589 Nm (435 lb ft) @ 3,400 rpm
Weight:	2,220 kg (4,885 lb)
Economy:	4.6 km/l (13 mpg)
Transmission:	GM TurboHydramatic automatic
Brakes:	Four wheel drums, 30.5 cm (12in) diameter
Body/chassis:	Steel body on steel X-frame chassis

UNITED STATES

CHEVROLET CORVAIR

Every car company wants its vehicles to make motoring history. Chevrolet's rear-engined compact Corvair achieved just that, but for all the wrong reasons.

Emulating the Volkswagen Beetle – seen as its main competition – the Corvair's engine was mounted at the back. The flat-six engine put it more in the Porsche 911 league though, especially when turbocharged in 1962. However, much of the engine was suspended behind the rear axle, creating a vehicle less well-balanced than the VW or Porsche, which lead to handling problems with the first cars.

1964 was the year of the major styling change. This is a 1966 model Corvair Corsa.

In 1965, a new suspension with upper and lower control arms was fitted to address handling questions.

The Corvair name is a blend of Corvette and Bel Air, both famous Chevy trademark names.

Customers could choose from a choice of 15 colours on the outside, and eight inside. A folding rag-top roof was a standard convertible option, but could be specified as power-operated.

All models of Corvair had neat, crisp styling. When the first cars appeared in October 1959, the trend on bigger cars was still towards flashy chrome and towering rear fins.

An air-cooled engine meant there was no need for a front grille.

UNITED STATES

A pparently, there is no such thing as bad publicity. Chevrolet during the 1960s would probably disagree. Having a whole chapter on the Corvair appear in a book entitled 'Unsafe at Any Speed' was not good for sales. Ironically, by the time Ralph Nader's attack appeared, the Corvair had been much improved.

In October 1959, the Big Three manufacturers all released compact cars to battle the wave of imports led by Volkswagen. Ford weighed in with the Falcon, Chrysler launched the Valiant, and Chevy launched the Corvair.

Of the three, the Corvair was by far the most fascinating, fitted with a rear-mounted

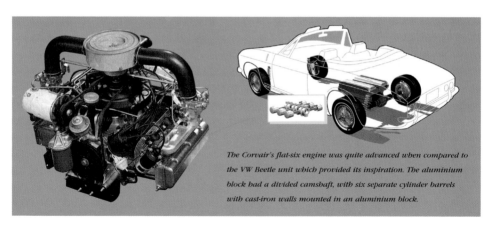

The Corvair's flat-six engine was quite advanced when compared to the VW Beetle unit which provided its inspiration. The aluminium block had a divided camshaft, with six separate cylinder barrels with cast-iron walls mounted in an aluminium block.

six-cylinder engine and displaying smart, uncluttered styling.

Porsche pretender

The car earned a reputation as 'a poor man's Porsche'. But then, it started to acquire a far less desirable image.

The Corvair suffered from oversteer, and in extreme cases would flip over on corners, the result was rear wheel tuck in. Chevrolet improved the suspension, but a high-profile accident in which comedian Eddie Kovacs was killed, and lawyer Ralph Nader's 1965 exposé on lax American safety standards, created a media backlash which decimated public confidence and sales.

Despite Chevrolet pointing out its suspension modifications and even demonstrating them using racing drivers, sales continued to fall. In 1969, Chevrolet pulled the plug.

The Corvair was totally vindicated by the National Highway Safety Administration in 1972, but it was all too late for one of America's most interesting cars.

Chevrolet Corvair (1966 turbocharged version)

Top speed:	185 km/h (115 mph)
0-96 km/h (0-60 mph):	10.8 secs
Engine type:	Flat-six
Displacement:	2,687 cc (164 ci)
Max power:	104 kW (140 bhp) @ 4,000 rpm
Max torque:	314 Nm (232 lb ft) @ 3,200 rpm
Weight:	1,236 kg (2,720 lb)
Economy:	9.9 km/l (28 mpg)
Transmission:	Three-speed manual, four-speed manual or optional two-speed automatic
Brakes:	Four-wheel drums
Body/chassis:	Integral chassis with two-door steel body

UNITED STATES

CHEVROLET CORVETTE STING RAY

Combine the brute force of a Chevrolet V8 with a fibreglass body, and you have one of America's favourite ever sports cars, the Corvette Sting Ray.

Sting Rays were built in convertible and coupé form. By far the most stylish variant of coupé was the 1963 version, with a split rear window. It looked great, but didn't help rear visibility much, so was dropped the next year.

Rear suspension was fully independent, unusual for an early 1960s American car. It's not an advanced set-up, but it works well.

The phenomenal performance of the Sting Ray meant that vented disc brakes were fitted from 1965. Previously, the car had been fitted with drums. However, if you wanted your Corvette on the cheap, you could still specify drum brakes to cut the price.

CHEVROLET CORVETTE STING RAY

The Sting Ray was the first American
production car to have rotating
headlamps since the 1942 De Soto. They
were operated by vacuum motors.

All Corvettes came with fibreglass
bodywork, fixed onto a steel skeleton
mounted on a traditional chassis.

Side exhausts were optional. They may have
looked cool, but as the pipes got very hot, they
had to be fitted with a protective frame to stop
burns to passengers and pedestrians. They were
also very noisy too.

UNITED STATES

79

hevrolet first launched the Corvette name in 1963, on a show car for the 1953 New York Motorama show. It was designed by styling guru Harvey Earl. The most noticeable feature of the attractive two-seater was its fibreglass body. Public interest convinced Chevrolet to put it into production, to compete against the Jaguar XK120 and, by 1955, the new Ford Thunderbird.

In 1961, there was a styling revision which pointed towards the Corvette's future shape. The trunk was smoothed off, altering the look of the back. A revamp of the rest of the car followed in 1963, transforming it into the angular-looking Sting Ray.

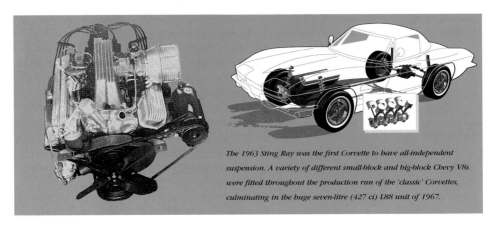

The 1963 Sting Ray was the first Corvette to have all-independent suspension. A variety of different small-block and big-block Chevy V8s were fitted throughout the production run of the 'classic' Corvettes, culminating in the huge seven-litre (427 ci) L88 unit of 1967.

The car was designed to be much more nimble than its predecessors, more European than American in feel. But the styling was planned to be like nothing else. The man in charge was Bill Mitchell, who based his ideas on the shape of a shark. It was an effective look: aggressive yet sleek, menacing yet aerodynamic.

Open or closed?

Sting Rays came in convertible and coupé form, the latter with a split rear screen, although this was soon altered. For racing, there was also the brusque-looking Grand Sport, although only five would be made.

The cars were subtly altered yearly, part of Chevrolet's programme of constant mechanical and cosmetic improvement.

The biggest change came in 1965 when disc brakes were (belatedly) fitted, just in time for the debut of the big-block Chevy V8 6,997 cc (427 ci) engine, with its massive 324 kW (435 bhp) output. When very different body styles came out in 1968, the Sting Ray was renamed 'Stingray'.

Chevrolet Corvette Sting Ray

Top speed:	217 km/h (135 mph)
0-96 km/h (0-60 mph):	5.6 secs
Engine type:	V8
Displacement:	6,997 cc (427 ci)
Max power:	324 kW (435 bhp) @ 6,200 rpm
Max torque:	623 Nm (460 lb ft) @ 4,000 rpm
Weight:	1,432 kg (3,150 lb)
Economy:	3.8 km/l (10 mpg)
Transmission:	Three-speed automatic, optional four-speed manual
Brakes:	Four-wheel vented discs with four-piston callipers (optional cast-iron drums)
Body/chassis:	Steel ladder frame with two-door convertible or coupé fibreglass body

UNITED STATES

CHEVROLET IMPALA

The bat-winged Impala was the pick of the late 1950s Chevrolet range. In 1959, only a Caddy could beat it for visual impact and utter flamboyance.

Engines ranged from a 3,867 cc (236 ci) in-line six, up to a triple carburettor 5,702 cc (348 ci) V8 with 235 kW (315 bhp). A fuel injected 4,638 cc (283 ci) V8 was a rare option in 1959.

The Impala in standard trim was long enough as it was, but with the addition of the Continental spare tyre cover, it grew a further 28 cm (11 in). Not having the wheel in the trunk made it capable of carrying vast amounts of luggage.

You got the most dramatic view of the Impala if you were following one. The 'cat's eye' tail lamps, huge deck lid and folded-over 'batwing' fins were among the wildest styling features to appear on any American car. While most other auto makers were going for height in 1959, Chevy went for width.

This 1959 Impala features many of the optional extras available to Chevrolet customers that year. It is fitted with side skirts, spot lights, the Continental spare tyre kit at the rear, bumper guards, cruise control, air-conditioning and a remote trunk release. And practically everything possible is electrically operated.

Initially, Chevrolet's Impala was not a model in its own right. It started life as the top option level on the Bel Air. Sales went up accordingly, so much so that for 1959, Chevrolet launched the name as a model in its own right.

And what a model. The Impala was by far the most ostentatious Chevrolet ever. This was the epoch of extravagant car design in the United States, but only Caddy went further than Chevy to create a flamboyant metal and chrome sculpture on wheels.

Impalas of this era came with a choice of engine options, from a puny 236 ci six-cylinder right up to a thunderous 5,702 cc (348 ci) V8. There was nothing radical about the V8s, which were of purely conventional construction with a central camshaft operating two valves per cylinder via pushrods and rockers.

The Impala was a wild-looking machine, long, wide and imposing. Available in three styles as a four-door sedan, two-door coupé and convertible coupé, each shared the same eye-catching looks. There was an overdose of chrome at the front, and the slab sides were punctuated by a large trim strip.

Bat fins and cat's eyes

The most excessive touches were saved for the rear though. While most other car firms opted for towering fins, Chevrolet simply folded them over so they were sticking out of the car's rear fenders. The effect was enhanced by the long and thin tail lamps. It would be impossible for anybody following an Impala to mistake it for anything else, even at night.

As well as an in-line six, there was the usual range of V8 engines available, as well as an unusual fuel injection option.

1959 marked the pinnacle of 1950s auto excess. For 1960, many cars were toned down, and the Impala was one of them, the distinct styling reined in, and the fuel injection disappearing. The name continued, but never again would it scale the styling heights of the '59 version.

Chevrolet Impala

Top speed:	216 km/h (134 mph)
0-96 km/h (0-60 mph):	9.0 secs
Engine type:	V8
Displacement:	5,702 cc (348 ci)
Max power:	235 kW (315 bhp) @ 5,600 rpm
Max torque:	484 Nm (357 lb ft) @ 3,600 rpm
Weight:	1,659 kg (3,657 lb)
Economy:	4.2 km/l (11.8 mpg)
Transmission:	Optional three- or four-speed manual or two-speed automatic
Brakes:	Four-wheel drums
Body/chassis:	Steel box-section cruciform chassis with two-door convertible body

UNITED STATES

85

CHRYSLER AIRFLOW

The aerodynamic Chrysler Airflow was a pioneering, revolutionary design in 1934. But it was too far ahead of its time and became a sales disaster.

The aerodynamic body came from wind tunnel tests, but was also developed with help from aviation pioneer Orville Wright. The construction technique was based on aircraft techniques, with the body mounted on beams and trusses. It was light but very strong.

Chrysler versions of the Airflow came with eight-cylinder engines, but De Soto-badged examples all came with six-cylinder units.

Five wheelbase lengths were available, up to the gargantuan 368 cm (145 in) Custom Imperials, which were so long, they almost looked as though they were bending in the middle.

Later model Imperials had innovative curved windshields, making the Airstream a pioneer in this field. Soon, this became an essential feature of car design.

The most noticeable feature of the Airflow was the plunging 'waterfall' grille. When the hoped-for sales failed to materialize, a more conventional 'skyscraper' grille was fitted for 1935. When that didn't do any good, the frontal style was again altered, as well as the trunk, but it failed to halt the decline.

Brakes were operated by hydraulics. Most competitors still used a rod or cable system to stop.

UNITED STATES

In 1927, Chrysler engineer Carl Breer watched a squadron of Army Air Corps combat planes flying low overhead. The sight inspired him to start thinking about incorporating aircraft styling and design into a car.

Scale models were tested in a wind tunnel and, following discussions with Orville Wright, a prototype called the Trifon Special was constructed in 1932. By 1934, this had become the production Airflow model.

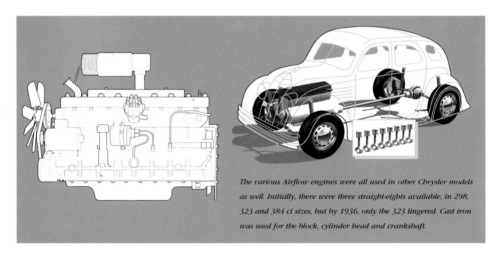

The various Airflow engines were all used in other Chrysler models as well. Initially, there were three straight-eights available, in 298, 323 and 384 ci sizes, but by 1936, only the 323 lingered. Cast iron was used for the block, cylinder head and crankshaft.

Chrysler expected great things of the streamlined Airflow, a real step forward in car design. Despite its innovation, the public remained unimpressed. The main criticisms levelled against the models were that they were clumsily executed and expensive.

Lack of success

Teething problems with the cars weren't helped by rival manufacturers running smear campaigns. In the first year, just 11,292 Chrysler Airflows were sold. The cheaper, but less well-specified De Soto models fared better, selling 13,940.

Despite a makeover for 1935, sales continued to fall. Chrysler even marketed a hood kit to transform a 1934 Airflow into a 1935 lookalike. But 1936 saw sales fall to 6,285 Airflows and 5,000 De Sotos.

There was one last attempt at altering the Airflow, in 1937. It didn't work, and the model was unceremoniously dropped in August of that year.

Ironically, the avant garde lines and engineering principles of the Airflow would soon be incorporated by Chrysler's rivals into their own models. And one of its fans was a young German engineer. His name was Ferdinand Porsche.

Chrysler Airflow

Top speed:	142 km/h (88 mph)
0-96 km/h (0-60mph):	19.5 secs
Engine type:	In-line eight
Displacement:	4,883 cc (298 ci)
Max power:	90 kW (122 bhp) @ 3,400 rpm
Max torque:	Not quoted
Weight:	1,894 kg (4,166 lb)
Economy:	5.7 km/l (16 mpg)
Transmission:	Three-speed manual
Brakes:	Front and rear drums
Body/chassis:	Steel girder chassis with four door steel sedan body

UNITED STATES

Citroën 2CV

Germany had the Volkswagen, Britain the Mini and France the 2CV, its own cheap and basic people's car that would prove to be exceptionally long-lived.

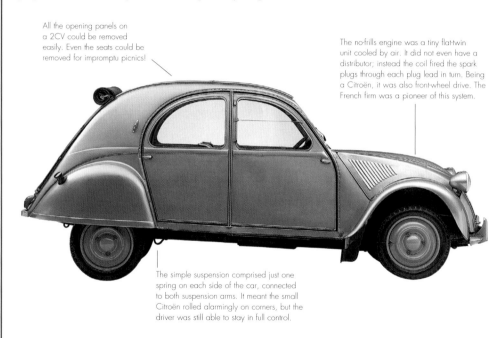

All the opening panels on a 2CV could be removed easily. Even the seats could be removed for impromptu picnics!

The no-frills engine was a tiny flat-twin unit cooled by air. It did not even have a distributor; instead the coil fired the spark plugs through each plug lead in turn. Being a Citroën, it was also front-wheel drive. The French firm was a pioneer of this system.

The simple suspension comprised just one spring on each side of the car, connected to both suspension arms. It meant the small Citroën rolled alarmingly on corners, but the driver was still able to stay in full control.

Until 1959, 2CVs were only available in grey, then blue became available. Green and yellow followed in 1960.

Fresh air motoring? No problem with a 2CV. Simply undo some pins and slide back the full canvas roof. If that isn't enough, there's even a flap on the lower section of the windshield.

The classic shape was penned by Flaminio Bertone who also went on to design the beautiful Citroën DS. The 2CV's shape was more functional though, intended to add stiffness to the shell.

91

Citroën 2CV

The origins of the 2CV date back to 1935, when Pierre Boulanger, chairman and managing director of the Citroën car company, dreamt up an idea for a car that would be able to transport four people and 50 kg (110 lb) of potatoes, or a barrel, at 60 km/h (37 mph), while achieving 20 km/l (56 mpg) fuel consumption figures. It also had to be capable of carrying a basket of eggs across a ploughed field without breaking any. Strange specifications indeed, but the

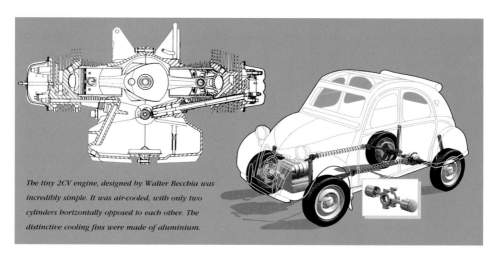

The tiny 2CV engine, designed by Walter Becchia was incredibly simple. It was air-cooled, with only two cylinders horizontally opposed to each other. The distinctive cooling fins were made of aluminium.

2CV was a basic car for a rural peasant population. Its main competition was the horse and cart.

The launch was delayed by World War II, and when the 2CV did eventually appear in 1948, it was to almost universal derision. It earned the nickname of the Tin Snail, others just called it the Duck.

Those who derided it did not understand. The 2CV was simple yet innovative, cheap but full of character. The masses it was intended to motorize took the eccentric French car to their hearts. Between 1948 and 1990, 5,114,920 cars would be produced. A major facelift in 1960 smoothed the body and updated the car, but it still kept its essential charm. From 1958 to 1966, you could even buy a version with four-wheel drive and two engines.

The classless Citroën

The 2CV didn't just appeal to its original target customer. It crossed all social boundaries, winning friends because of its quirky nature and terrific sense of fun. Today, this unpretentious little French car has many devoted followers and enthusiasts' clubs and associations can be found all over the world.

Citroën 2CV

Top speed:	66 km/h (41 mph)
0-96 km/h (0-60mph):	n/a
Engine type:	Flat-twin
Displacement:	375 cc (23 ci)
Max power:	6.7 kW (9 bhp) @ 3,500 rpm
Max torque:	22 Nm (16 lb ft) @ 1,800 rpm
Weight:	500 kg (1,100 lb)
Economy:	22.3 km/l (63 mpg)
Transmission:	Four-speed manual
Brakes:	Four-wheel drums
Body/chassis:	Separate chassis with four-door steel sedan body

FRANCE

CITROËN SM

What happens when the talents of France's most innovative manufacturer combine with the expertise of a top Italian engine builder? You get the SM supercar.

The SM shape was typically Citroën, updating the lines of the classic DS for the 1970s and adding a hatchback. SM stood for Serie Maserati.

The quad-cam V6 in the SM was based on the Maserati's V8 unit. There were initial plans to use the V8, but it was found to be much too powerful for front-wheel drive and would have made the hood too long.

Citroën's traditional self-levelling hydropneumatic suspension was continued on the SM. It meant a soft, smooth ride, but resulted in lots of body roll during fast cornering. Ride heights could be set from inside the cabin.

Six headlamps dominated the front of the SM, the inner ones being linked to the steering so they would turn when going around corners. They were also self-levelling.

Power-assisted steering was powerful at low speeds, but assistance deliberately declined as the car went faster. The strong self-centring of the steering wheel took many novice drivers by surprise.

Power brakes were linked to the hydraulic system, meaning they were incredibly sensitive. Just a small amount of foot pressure could invoke a rubber-shredding emergency stop.

FRANCE

95

itroën had wanted a prestigious, powerful flagship for years, but plans to fit a six-cylinder engine to its DS sedan hadn't materialized. Then, in 1966, an agreement was reached with the Italian Maserati firm to build a V6 engine. When Citroën bought a controlling stake in the firm two years later, it was effectively the green light to start work on its own GT sedan.

The result was the SM in 1970. A glorious blend of smooth power, quirky engineering and sleek angular styling with a brooding,

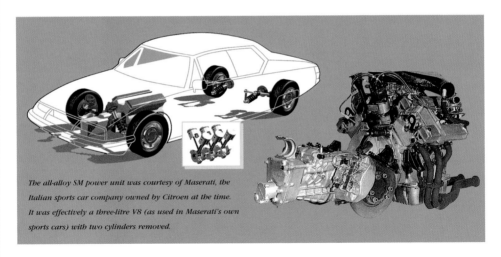

The all-alloy SM power unit was courtesy of Maserati, the Italian sports car company owned by Citroen at the time. It was effectively a three-litre V8 (as used in Maserati's own sports cars) with two cylinders removed.

almost sinister appearance, it was a technical tour de force. The interior looked like it was designed to be as bizarre as possible, with oval instruments, odd-shaped controls and a single-spoke steering wheel.

It looked fantastic, but there were problems. Because of the hurried development, the engine was unreliable and difficult to keep in tune, fuel consumption was appalling, ventilation was poor, accommodation was cramped and the hydraulic steering and brakes were difficult to get used to.

French finale

Despite press adulation and the adoption of fuel injection to improve reliability, economy and performance, desperately needed sales in America didn't happen. So when Citroën was sold to Peugeot in 1974, the SM was destined to be dropped.

The new owners sold Maserati in May 1975, and immediately stopped SM manufacture. Hundreds of partially completed bodyshells were ordered to be sent to the crusher. It was the end of the road for one of the world's most distinctive and individual cars.

Citroën SM

Top speed:	229 km/h (142 mph)
0-96 km/h (0-60 mph):	8.5 secs
Engine type:	V6
Displacement:	2,769 cc (169 ci)
Max power:	133 kW (178 bhp) @ 5,500 rpm
Max torque:	232 Nm (171 lb ft) @ 4,000 rpm
Weight:	1,453 kg (3,197 lb)
Economy:	4.4 km/l (12.4 mpg)
Transmission:	Five-speed manual
Brakes:	Four-wheel discs
Body/chassis:	Unitary construction with two-door, four-seat hatchback body

FRANCE

97

CORD 810/812

The Cord 810/812 was built to a limited time scale and with severe financial restraints, yet became one of America's most striking vehicles ever.

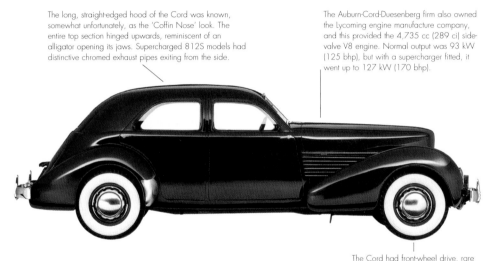

The long, straight-edged hood of the Cord was known, somewhat unfortunately, as the 'Coffin Nose' look. The entire top section hinged upwards, reminiscent of an alligator opening its jaws. Supercharged 812S models had distinctive chromed exhaust pipes exiting from the side.

The Auburn-Cord-Duesenberg firm also owned the Lycoming engine manufacture company, and this provided the 4,735 cc (289 ci) side-valve V8 engine. Normal output was 93 kW (125 bhp), but with a supercharger fitted, it went up to 127 kW (170 bhp).

The Cord had front-wheel drive, rare for any car of this era, let alone an American one. It was inspired by the Citroën Traction Avant, launched a year before the 810/812 range.

Dashboard design was inspired by aviation styling, with the instruments set into a shiny alloy panel. Some of the dials inside were even triangular.

The streamlined art deco body was a masterpiece from designer Gordon Beuhrig, later to become an aircraft stylist.

Pop-up headlamps were a Cord innovation. They were operated by a manual handle on the dashboard. The light units themselves were adapted from aircraft landing lights.

UNITED STATES

UNITED STATES

Errett Lobban Cord was known as 'the boy wonder of the automobile industry' in the 1930s. In 1924, he bought the struggling Auburn Automobile Company and then embarked on a series of motoring and aviation acquisitions, including Duesenberg in 1926, ultimately forming the Cord Corporation in 1929.

The original concept behind the car which was to become the Cord 810/812 was to produce a baby Duesenberg. It was to be a highly advanced car, with front-wheel drive, a specially manufactured V8 engine, and radical bodywork for the era. Its stylist was the free-thinking Gordon Beuhrig, who incorporated a number of novel ideas into

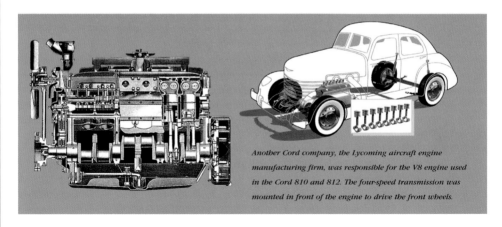

Another Cord company, the Lycoming aircraft engine manufacturing firm, was responsible for the V8 engine used in the Cord 810 and 812. The four-speed transmission was mounted in front of the engine to drive the front wheels.

his futuristic creation, including retractable headlamps, operated from inside the cabin.

Design revelation

In 1935, the Duesenberg appeared as a Cord instead. It was developed on a strict budget, and in a very short space of time. Considering these limitations, it's amazing the car turned out as astonishing as it was. At shows, the Cord 810 stole the limelight above everything else.

Deliveries began in 1936. It sold well, if not spectacularly, but behind the scenes, the company that made it was starting to self-destruct. Soon, it found itself struggling to put right the teething problems many new owners were facing.

For 1937, the car was renamed the 812, with some minor modifications incorporated. Big news though was the appearance of a supercharger, to create the 812S, at last giving the Cord the power and performance its looks demanded.

It was to no avail though. Production of one of America's most imaginative cars stopped later that year, due to crippling financial problems. The car may have been great, but its builder wasn't.

Cord 810/812

Top speed:	145 km/h (90 mph)
0-96 km/h (0-60 mph):	20.0 secs
Engine type:	V8
Displacement:	4,735 cc (289 ci)
Max power:	93 kW (125 bhp) @ 3,500 rpm
Max torque:	Not quoted
Weight:	1,659 kg (3,657 lb)
Economy:	5.3 km/l (15 mpg)
Transmission:	Four-speed pre-selector
Brakes:	Four-wheel drums, 30.5 cm (12 in) diameter
Body/chassis:	Separate steel box-section chassis with four-door sedan body

UNITED STATES

Datsun 240Z

The 240Z opened the floodgates for Japanese sports cars. Everything about it, from price to performance, was exciting, and was matched by huge sales success.

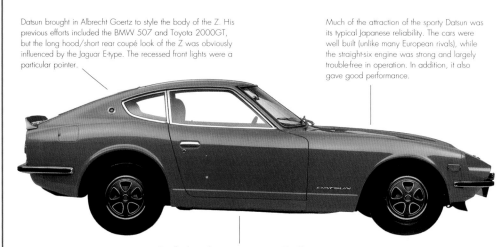

Datsun brought in Albrecht Goertz to style the body of the Z. His previous efforts included the BMW 507 and Toyota 2000GT, but the long hood/short rear coupé look of the Z was obviously influenced by the Jaguar E-type. The recessed front lights were a particular pointer.

Much of the attraction of the sporty Datsun was its typical Japanese reliability. The cars were well built (unlike many European rivals), while the straight-six engine was strong and largely trouble-free in operation. In addition, it also gave good performance.

An all-independent suspension, using MacPherson struts at the front and Chapman struts at the rear, meant that the 240Z handled superbly. Its cornering abilities were worthy of a much more expensive sports car.

Unlike many sports cars of the era, a convertible version was never built.

A hatchback was a useful feature, enhancing the practicality of the 240Z, although space inside wasn't great, thanks to the spare tyre and struts. Not all cars had a rear spoiler fitted.

One penny-pinching aspect of the 240Z was the wheels, which were just fitted with cheap-looking 'alloy effect' wheel trims.

JAPAN

103

DATSUN 240Z

At the end of the 1960s, European manufacturers must have felt they had the American sports car market completely sewn up. There was little incentive for companies like Triumph and MG to try harder when no one else seemed able to mount a reasonable challenge.

Nobody expected a competitor to come from the Far East. Yet when Datsun launched the 240Z in 1969, it was a runaway success, redefining the concept of what made an affordable but effective sports car.

The Japanese car industry had been growing in stature since 1945, but there

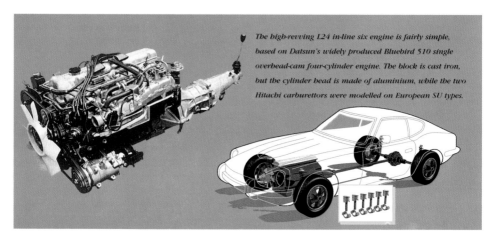

The high-revving L24 in-line six engine is fairly simple, based on Datsun's widely produced Bluebird 510 single overhead-cam four-cylinder engine. The block is cast iron, but the cylinder head is made of aluminium, while the two Hitachi carburettors were modelled on European SU types.

had been no successful sports model that had managed to appeal to a worldwide audience. The 240Z was developed entirely with export in mind. In particular, it was aimed at the lucrative US marketplace, to battle the best Europe could offer.

All in one package

Datsun had a strong package with the 240Z. It blended smooth, perfectly proportioned lines by Count Albrecht Goertz with simple but dependable Japanese mechanics and a highly competitive price. Its price was the same as Triumph GT6, yet the Japanese car offered so much more. Performance was good, with few of the dramas associated with its opposition, and the Z car was also blessed with outstanding handling, thanks to its all-independent suspension. Perhaps its only major fault was one shared by most Japanese cars of the era – a tendency to rust badly. But that certainly wasn't a problem confined solely to cars from the Far East.

The original 240Z lasted for five years, before it was replaced by the 260Z, with a bigger engine, but less class. The ultimate development of the Z shape was the 280ZX, which was larger, slower and less fun.

Datsun 240Z

Top speed:	201 km/h (125 mph)
0-96 km/h (0-60 mph):	8.7 secs
Engine type:	In-line six
Displacement:	2,393 cc (146 ci)
Max power:	112 kW (150 bhp) @ 6,000 rpm
Max torque:	201 Nm (148 lb ft) @ 4,400 rpm
Weight:	1,070 kg (2,355 lb)
Economy:	8.9 km/l (25 mpg)
Transmission:	Four- or five-speed manual or three-speed automatic
Brakes:	Discs at front, drums at rear
Body/chassis:	Steel monocoque with two-door coupé body

JAPAN

105

DeLorean DMC-12

The DeLorean's gleaming, futuristic appearance made it the star of three time-travelling movies. But the truth behind the shine was more down to earth.

To keep costs down, the DMC-12 used an all-alloy V6 engine, developed by Peugeot/Renault/Volvo. Although the unit was quite powerful in the European cars, it had to be detuned so much for the American market that the DeLorean was uncompetitively slow compared to its rivals.

The DeLorean's distinctive external appearance came from its stainless steel-clad panels, covering a Vacuum Assisted Resin Injection bodyshell. They not only added extra weight to the car, but made it difficult to keep clean too. The steel would show fingerprints easily, and the DeLorean company even supplied special cleaning materials with every car sold.

Conventional electric windows weren't fitted. Instead, there was a small cut-out in the door glass.

Gullwing doors were influenced by the Mercedes-Benz 300SL, but were a handy marketing gimmick as well.

The DeLorean designer was Giorgetti Giugiaro, who had also designed the Lotus Esprit. The two have similar lines.

The DeLorean was rear-engined, and had larger tyres at the rear than at the front. 65 per cent of the car's weight was over the back wheels.

'Where we're going, we don't need roads!' Those words, spoken about the DeLorean DMC-12 time machine in 1985's *Back to the Future* assured the car immortality and desirability. What a pity for John DeLorean that the car had gone out of production in 1982.

DeLorean was one of the flamboyant stars of General Motors when he walked out in 1973, planning to build an 'ethical' sports car that would seem fresh and innovative for years to come.

Giorgetti Giugiaro of Ital Design came up with the car design, while DeLorean raised

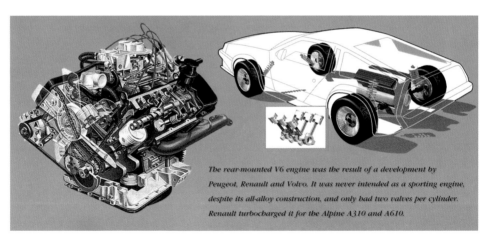

The rear-mounted V6 engine was the result of a development by Peugeot, Renault and Volvo. It was never intended as a sporting engine, despite its all-alloy construction, and only had two valves per cylinder. Renault turbocharged it for the Alpine A310 and A610.

money selling dealer franchises. There were plans to build the factory in Puerto Rico, until the British government gave £94 million ($141 million) in loans and grants to set up a plant in Northern Ireland.

Lotus input

However, all was not well. Lotus boss Colin Chapman was brought in to develop the DMC-12 and was horrified by what he found. The Lotus team kept the basic look of the car, but substituted an Esprit-type backbone chassis to improve handling and strength.

Production started in 1980, but build quality was poor and performance on the American cars was disappointing, thanks to Federal emissions regulations. It was also very expensive. The company started to lose money badly.

In February 1982, the firm went into receivership, just a week before John DeLorean was arrested on drugs charges.

He was eventually acquitted, but there was no reprieve for his car. 2000 were left unsold when the company folded.

DeLorean DMC-12

Top speed:	201 k/h (125 mph)
0-96 km/h (0-60 mph):	9.6 secs
Engine type:	V6
Displacement:	2,850 cc (174 ci)
Max power:	108 kW (145 bhp) @ 5,500 rpm
Max torque:	220 Nm (162 lb ft) @ 2,750 rpm
Weight:	1,291 kg (2,840 lb)
Economy:	6 km/l (17 mpg)
Transmission:	Renault-derived five-speed manual
Brakes:	Four wheel discs, 26.7 cm (10.5 in) diameter at front, 25.4 cm (10 in) diameter at rear
Body/chassis:	Sheet-steel backbone chassis with fibreglass coupé body covered with stainless steel

UNITED KINGDOM

DE TOMASO PANTERA

The peculiar but successful combination of an Argentinian racing driver, Italian engineering and American muscle resulted in the long-lived and brutal De Tomaso Pantera.

The optional large rear spoiler aided stability, but also slowed the Pantera down. During tests, cars without wings were proved to be fractionally faster, but more difficult to control.

The engine was a mid-mounted Ford V8 rated at 5,763 cc (352 ci), previously used in the Ford Mustang.

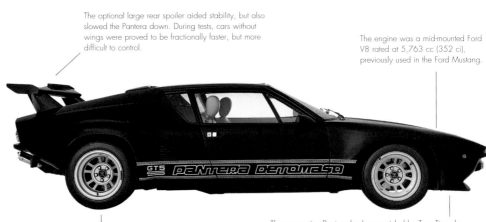

With power being transmitted through the rear wheels, the rear tyres were larger than those fitted at the front.

The aggressive Pantera body was styled by Tom Tjaarda, with Giampaolo Dallara (one of the names behind the Lamborghini Miura) responsible for the structural design. This teaming created a steel monocoque car intended for large-scale production, as Ford intended.

Rear visibility was appalling, even without the rear wing in place. With it installed, you just had to cross your fingers and trust in your wing mirrors.

Extra driving lights could be fitted in the front spoiler, and were a useful fitting considering the poor reputation of the Italian electrics and the headlamps.

The five-speed transaxle had proven supercar heritage, having also been used in the Ford GT40.

ITALY

111

There's nothing that subtle about a De Tomaso Pantera. Imagine a typical American muscle car styled with Italian flair, but made suitable for mass production and you have some idea of what the Pantera was all about.

Alejandro De Tomaso was an Argentinian racing driver who fled his home country, and eventually established his own company in the heartland of Italian supercar production at Modena.

The first De Tomaso road car was the Vallelunga in 1965, followed by the Mangusta in 1967. Both had mid-mounted Ford engines, so were known to Blue Oval chiefs.

Out of the blue, De Tomaso got a call from Ford asking if he was interested in collaborating on a replacement for the

Various Ford V8 engines were fitted to the Pantera throughout its long life, but the best was arguably the 'Cleveland' 5,763 cc (352 ci) unit from 1974. This high-lift camshaft powerhouse was very tuneable, and was quite lightweight, thanks to the thin wall-casting.

Shelby Mustang. The mastermind was Ford's Lee Iacocca, who had also been responsible for the Mustang.

Italian-American hybrid

The 1971 Pantera, with its mid-mounted Ford V8, was engineered to be simple to put together, with the aim of selling around 5,000 cars a year, mainly in the US. Ford provided funds to develop the dramatic-looking affordable supercar, the deal being that it would retain distribution rights in America, while De Tomaso handled the European side.

Quality control problems were evident from the start, but Ford persevered, hoping for a success that would never come. As the 1970s became more energy conscious, Ford decided it had had enough and pulled out.

That didn't stop the Pantera though. De Tomaso simply carried on limited production on its own. The cars moved into more conventional supercar territory, especially with the GT5 of 1982, with

enormous wheel arch extensions, front air dam and rear wing.

A restyle in 1990 smoothed the car's looks and a turbocharger was also added.

De Tomaso Pantera

Top speed:	266 km/h (165 mph)
0-96 km/h (0-60 mph):	5.6 secs
Engine type:	V8
Displacement:	5,763 cc (352 ci)
Max power:	261 kW (350 bhp) @ 6,000 rpm
Max torque:	451 Nm (333 lb ft) @ 3,800 rpm
Weight:	1,463 kg (3,219 lb)
Economy:	4.6 km/l (13 mpg)
Transmission:	ZF five-speed manual transaxle
Brakes:	Four-wheel vented discs, 29.7 cm (11.7 in) diameter at front, 28.4 cm (11.2 in) diameter at rear
Body/chassis:	Steel monocoque two-door, two-seat coupé

ITALY

DODGE CHARGER

The Ford Mustang and the Plymouth Barracuda popularized the fastback muscle car in the mid-1960s. Dodge's answer was the mighty Charger.

Rear buttresses were a distinctive styling feature, but were also needed to stiffen the pillarless coupé roof.

There were seven different power outputs from the V8 engines. Top choice was the Hemi unit, which could produce 317 kW (425 bhp).

The Charger's dynamic star quality meant it often featured on TV and in the movies. Its most notable performances were in *The Dukes of Hazzard* and *Bullitt*, where it was the car chased by Frank Bullitt's Mustang through San Francisco.

Front disc brakes were only ever an option on the 1968 to 1970 versions, even the ones with the most potent performance. Having to stop quickly was always slightly difficult in a Charger.

The R/T badge stands for 'Road/Track' and signifies this car was fitted with Dodge's popular performance upgrade option, featuring the biggest Chrysler engine available at the time, a 7,210 cc (440 ci) V8.

A Charger trademark was the lights concealed behind the full-length grille. The covers are hinged.

Rear suspension was basic leaf-spring technology. Faster models had six springs, other Chargers just had four.

I n 1964, the Mustang changed American history. It was the original personal muscle car, and was such a runaway success – over a million sold in less than two years – that other US manufacturers rushed to follow its lead.

Dodge had showcased a Charger concept car in 1965, to measure public reaction to the fastback body design. The results were favourable, so it launched the slightly altered production version the following year, as its entry in the muscle car hall of fame.

The Charger was a much bigger car than its Ford rival, based on the mid-sized Coronet platform. It was singularly styled by Dodge's design chief Bill Brownlie, with hidden headlamps and sweeping C pillars, supporting the pillarless roof.

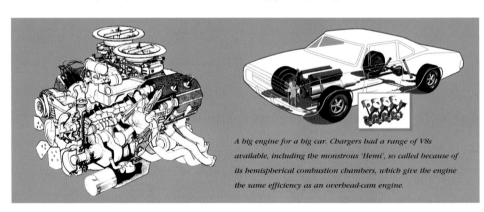

A big engine for a big car. Chargers had a range of V8s available, including the monstrous 'Hemi', so called because of its hemispherical combustion chambers, which give the engine the same efficiency as an overhead-cam engine.

The classic Charger shape came in 1968, with more curvaceous lines and a recessed rear screen between two buttresses. The shape was menacing, but also beguiling, and resulted in sales six times those of the 1967 model. The most extreme Chargers could be specified with Chrysler's all-conquering 426 V8 Hemi, the powerhouse of choice for anybody serious about street or drag racing.

Daytona dynamite

The most outrageous Charger appeared in 1969. Intended for NASCAR racing, the Daytona was a stretched Charger, with a smoothed-off pointed nose and high rear spoiler. It was extreme both in looks and performance: on the track, it could top 241 km/h (150 mph).

Styling changed again in 1971, but not for the better. The pure lines of Chargers past became cluttered and garish, and engines were detuned as emissions laws began to bite. The name continued, but the magic had disappeared, living on in the many celluloid appearances by one of America's greatest ever muscle cars.

Dodge Charger

Top speed:	266 km/h (165 mph)
0-96 km/h (0-60 mph):	7.5 secs
Engine type:	V8
Displacement:	7,210 cc (440 ci)
Max power:	298 kW (400 bhp) @ 4,800 rpm
Max torque:	556 Nm (410 lb ft) @ 3,600 rpm
Weight:	1,625 kg (3,574 lb)
Economy:	3.8 km/l (10.7 mpg)
Transmission:	Three-speed TorqueFlite automatic
Brakes:	Four-wheel drums, 27.9 cm (11 in) diameter at front, 25.4 cm (10 in) diameter at rear
Body/chassis:	Unitary construction with additional ladder frame and two-door pillarless coupé body

UNITED STATES

DODGE VIPER

The Dodge Viper started life as a concept car. But public reaction made it a production reality and turned it into an American motoring icon.

The roll bar (on convertibles) is stylishly built into the structure of the car.

The Viper is the world's only production car with a V10 engine. It also has the distinction of having the largest, at eight litres or 488 ci, capable of pushing out over 298 kW (400 bhp). Construction is all-alloy.

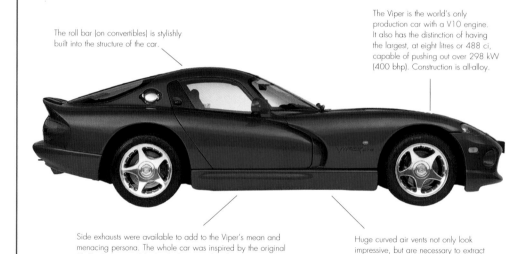

Side exhausts were available to add to the Viper's mean and menacing persona. The whole car was inspired by the original Shelby Cobra, and the body design, with its long nose and stubby tail, took distinct styling cues from the earlier racing legend.

Huge curved air vents not only look impressive, but are necessary to extract hot air from the engine.

The six-speed transmission is a Borg-Warner unit, specially designed to handle the huge torque of the Dodge. It electronically changes from first to fourth automatically under light throttle.

According to Dodge, the design of these headlamps is 'aero-polyellipsoid' – teardrop-shaped.

The lightweight body is of plastic composite construction, which is surprisingly tough in the event of an accident.

Wheels and tyres are different sizes front and rear to aid handling.

UNITED STATES

In the late 1980s, the Chrysler corporation found itself with a new president. Bob Lutz had been a former executive vice-president of Ford, but more importantly, he was a real car enthusiast.

The new man set about reshaping Chrysler's somewhat tarnished image. One of his first and most dramatic moves was to commission the design of a concept car for the 1989 motor show circuit. He enlisted chairman Lee Iacocca, stylist Tom Gale, chief engineer Francois Castaing and all-round racing legend Carroll Shelby to help produce what he envisaged as being a Cobra for the 1990s. The result was the outrageous Viper.

The Viper is the only production car to utilize a V10 engine. It is a massively powerful all-alloy unit, developed by that Italian master of engine art, Lamborghini. The 488 ci engine equates to almost eight litres, and can pump out well over 298 kW (400 bbp).

Even down to its serpent-inspired name, the Viper was an unashamed tribute to the iconic Cobra. It was a monstrous two-seater, equipped with a demonic V10 engine, and capable of phenomenal speeds. Everything about it was over-the-top – practicality was never a consideration. After all, this car was not going to be made...

Concept into reality

Except that when the American public saw the Viper, they adored it and clamoured for it to go into production. Chrysler happily agreed, and in 1990, Iacocca announced the car would go on sale in 1992.

In the energy, safety and money conscious 1990s, there were many arguments against such a hedonistic car. There was just one reason for it to be built: because it was extravagant fun. And that was all the excuse that was needed. It was an uncompromising brute, but one which was incredible to drive in the right circumstances.

The Viper is still in production today, now available as both an open car and a coupé. And it's just as ludicrously wonderful as ever.

Dodge Viper

Top speed:	261 km/h (162 mph)
0-96 km/h: (0-60 mph):	5.4 secs
Engine type:	V10
Displacement:	7,998 cc (488 ci)
Max power:	298 kW (400 bhp) @ 4,600 rpm
Max torque:	661 Nm (488 lb ft) @ 3,600 rpm
Weight:	1,580 kg (3,477 lb)
Economy:	4.3 km/l (12 mpg)
Transmission:	Six-speed manual with electronic shift lockout
Brakes:	Four-wheel vented discs, 33.0 cm (13 in) diameter
Body/chassis:	Tubular-steel chassis with two-seat fibreglass reinforced plastic convertible or coupé body

UNITED STATES

121

Edsel

The Edsel was motoring's equivalent of the Titanic, a disaster of epic proportions for Ford. But did the car really deserve its reputation and fate?

Vinyl soft-tops on Citations came in four colours: black, white, copper and turquoise. Naturally, they were power-operated.

Ninety two per cent of Edsels came with automatic transmission. There was also the option of Teletouch transmission, controlled by push buttons in the centre of the steering wheel. It was more of a gimmick than a reliable system.

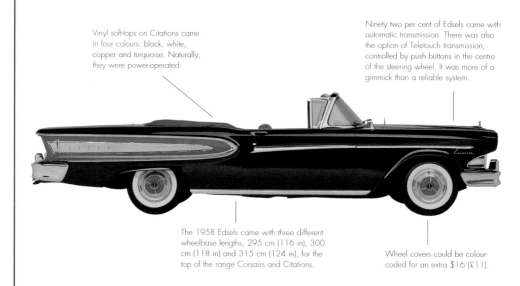

The 1958 Edsels came with three different wheelbase lengths, 295 cm (116 in), 300 cm (118 in) and 315 cm (124 in), for the top of the range Corsairs and Citations.

Wheel covers could be colour-coded for an extra $16 (£11).

Edsel buyers could choose 161 different colour combinations, including contrasting two-tone schemes.

Styling – both inside and out – was over-the-top even by 1950s American standards, and came at a time when car buyers were turning away from garish extravaganza towards restraint.

The vertical grille was the feature that came in for most criticism. Designer Roy Brown referred to it as 'combining nostalgia with modern vertical thrust'. Others called it a horse collar, a toilet seat, even an Oldsmobile sucking a lemon. The shape would be toned down every year.

UNITED STATES

dsel Ford was Henry Ford's only son. He is chiefly remembered for the car named after him which became one of the most expensive and embarrassing automotive failures of all time. It was also a vehicle he had nothing to do with.

Edsel the man died in 1943. Edsel the car was born in 1957 and died in 1959, after a troubled and turbulent existence. In the mid-1950s, Ford decided to create a new range to try and battle General Motor's market dominance. There were 18,000 recommendations for a new name, but Ford chairman Ernest Breech ignored them all, choosing Edsel in tribute to the former company president.

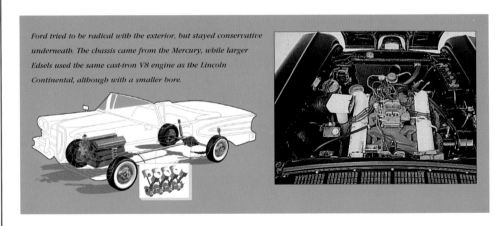

Ford tried to be radical with the exterior, but stayed conservative underneath. The chassis came from the Mercury, while larger Edsels used the same cast-iron V8 engine as the Lincoln Continental, although with a smaller bore.

Meanwhile, the car itself was undergoing development by noted stylist Roy Brown. He reversed the usual concept seen on almost all big American cars of the time of wide grilles and towering fins, giving the Edsel a vertical grille and folded-over fins. 18 models would eventually be launched, in four different series: the Ranger, the Pacer, the Corsair and the most expensive, the Citation.

Edsel's end

But it would be all too much for customers. The styling, combined with poor build quality and a recession, meant that projected sales failed to materialize. The looks became a national joke.

Ford toned down the design, but it did little good as the damage had already been done. In 1959, the controversial styling was dropped altogether, and the cars became little more than rebadged Ford Galaxies. It was to no avail. Just a month later, the Edsel was discontinued altogether. In total, Ford had lost around $400 million (£270 million).

Ironically, Edsels today are very desirable because of their originality and character.

Edsel

Top speed:	169 km/h (105 mph)
0-96 km/h (0-60 mph):	9.7 secs
Engine type:	V8
Displacement:	6,719 cc (410 ci)
Max power:	257 kW (345 bhp) @ 4,600 rpm
Max torque:	643 Nm (475 lb ft) @ 2,900 rpm
Weight:	1,960 kg (4,311 lb)
Economy:	3.5 km/l (10 mpg)
Transmission:	Three-speed automatic
Brakes:	Four-wheel drums, 27.9 cm (11 in) diameter
Body/chassis:	Separate curbed perimeter chassis frame with centre X-brace body

UNITED STATES

FACEL VEGA

Outrageously expensive, superbly luxurious and flamboyantly French, the Facel Vega with its V8 Chrysler engine was a charismatic throwback to a different age of motoring.

No rear passengers, but lots of luggage? No problem. The rear seats folded down into a handy platform, although the boot was big enough to carry practically anything.

V8s of varying sizes were supplied by Chrysler to power the bigger Facel Vegas. In fact, it was only when the company steered away from this formula, building the smaller Facellia with its own design of twin-cam engine, that Facel ran into financial trouble and collapsed.

The Facel Vega came with Michelin X tyres as standard fitments. They had a claimed safe speed limit of 190 km/h (118 mph), which was rather worrying if you took one of these cars up to its maximum speed of 225 km/h (140 mph)!

This car is a Facel Vega II, the 1961 restyled version of the HK500. The wraparound windshield was narrower, the roof line was lower, the trunk was made larger and there were many other cosmetic changes, including stacked front headlamps. Only 184 cars of this style were made.

Disc brakes were adopted from 1960. Before this, finned alloy drums were the way to stop a Vega.

FRANCE

127

When you are one of the world's greatest racing drivers, used to driving some of the planet's fastest and most exotic machines, which car do you choose as your own personal transport? In the case of British racing star Stirling Moss, he chose the French-made Facel Vega.

The list of past famous Facel owners is an exclusive one. As well as Moss, Pablo Picasso, Ringo Starr, Tony Curtis and Ava Gardner all drove examples of this exotic French marque. They were among the few who could afford to.

The Facel firm was founded in 1939, initially building bodies for other auto

Facel Vega bought in all of its V8 engines from Chrysler. By 1960, the engine of choice was the cast-iron pushrod Chrysler 383 V8 of 6,286 cc (383 ci). It was hugely powerful, but far from economical.

manufacturers. In 1954, it constructed its own vehicle, the Vega. The handsome-looking and extravagant creation, with dramatic front, was powered by a Chrysler V8, which could power the heavy vehicle up to 185 km/h (115 mph) and beyond, as engine capacity gradually increased over the next few years. It was stylish but expensive.

Big, bigger, biggest...

An ordinary Vega was imposing, but in 1956 came the pillarless Excellence limousine, measuring 5.2 metres (17 ft) long. Its size was matched by its cost, but there were few cars which could beat it for performance and luxury at the time.

The Vega was re-engineered into the HK500 in 1958, and made more elaborate, both inside and out. The Facel Vega II followed a couple of years later, and by this time, the hood hid a monstrous Chrysler 383 V8 engine. It was claimed to be the world's fastest sedan.

All Facels died in 1964 when the firm failed, due mainly to the unreliability of its smaller Facellia car.

Facel Vega

Top speed:	225 km/h (140 mph)
0-96 km/h (0-60 mph):	8.6 secs
Engine type:	V8
Displacement:	6,286 cc (383 ci)
Max power:	291 kW (390 bhp) @ 5,200 rpm
Max torque:	577 Nm (425 lb ft) @ 3,000 rpm
Weight:	1,833 kg (4,033 lb)
Economy:	3.7 km/l (10.4 mpg)
Transmission:	Four-speed manual
Brakes:	Four-wheel discs, 30.5 cm (12 in) diameter at front, 29.2 cm (11.5 in) diameter at rear
Body/chassis:	Separate tubular steel chassis with steel pillarless two-door sedan body

FRANCE

FERRARI DAYTONA

The Daytona marked the end of traditional front-engined Ferraris. It may have been the end of a great era, but what a way to go...

The Daytona was almost perfectly balanced. With the V12 set back in the chassis, and the transmission to the rear, weight distribution was 52:48. The gearbox shared the same alloy housing as the final drive.

A nice but subtle feature was the Ferrari prancing horse badge picked out on the wraparound front indicators. After the Daytona's launch, this fashion statement would be much-copied by other manufacturers.

The outer shell was a blend of steel and alloy. The doors, hood and bootlid were all aluminium, everything else was steel. Beneath the panels was a framework of chrome-molybdenum tubes welded together to give great structural integrity. This arrangement also made the car heavy, though.

The sublime body styling was one of Pininfarina's greatest masterpieces.

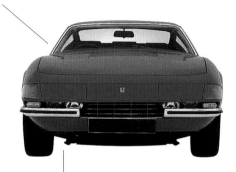

The model designation for the Daytona is the 365 GTB/4. The '365' signifies the size of each cylinder, which when multiplied by the number of cylinders (in this case, 12) gives the displacement in litres. The '4' stands for the number of camshafts.

Front headlamps could be raised in three seconds, as specified by American safety regulations.

ITALY

131

Officially, it was never called the Daytona. The real designation for Ferrari's late 1960s supercar was the 365 GTB/4. But when the media first saw the latest Italian stunner at the 1968 Paris Motor Show, it was immediately christened the Daytona in honour of Ferrari's success in the famous American 24-hour race the year before.

As was usual with Ferraris, the Daytona came with Pininfarina styling and the customary V12 engine. However, Pininfarina's smooth yet purposeful fastback styling was one of his best sculptures, while the V12 engine developed a hair-raising 262 kW (352 bhp). It was a complicated creation, with four camshafts and six twin-choke carburettors making it difficult to tune.

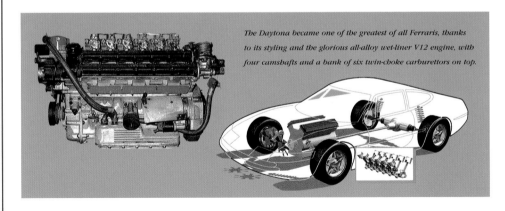

The Daytona became one of the greatest of all Ferraris, thanks to its styling and the glorious all-alloy wet-liner V12 engine, with four camshafts and a bank of six twin-choke carburettors on top.

Sublime savage

As exquisite as it may have looked and sounded, the Daytona was frighteningly savage on the road. It was meant to be driven fast, so much so that it became difficult to drive at anything less than 193 km/h (120 mph). Still, as the fastest production car of its day, it was easy to reach such speeds. Press the accelerator hard from rest and the car would reach 161 km/h (100 mph) in under 13 seconds. Driven hard and quick, it was utterly exhilarating.

As well as the coupé, stylish convertible versions were also available when the Daytona went into production in 1969, plus astonishingly quick competition models.

Even when new though, the Daytona was an anachronism. Lamborghini had shown the way forward for supercars with its mid-engined Miura, and Ferrari was forced to play catchup. In 1973, the 365 GT4 BB replacement for the Daytona had its engine fixed amidships.

The Daytona went into the history books as a front-engined swansong of epic proportions.

Ferrari Daytona

Top speed:	280 km/h (174 mph)
0-96 km/h (0-60 mph):	5.6 secs
Engine type:	V12
Displacement:	4,390 cc (268 ci)
Max power:	262 kW (352 bhp) @ 7,500 rpm
Max torque:	577 Nm (425 lb ft) @ 5,500 rpm
Weight:	1605 kg (3,530 lb)
Economy:	4.2 km/l (11.8 mpg)
Transmission:	Rear mounted five-speed manual
Brakes:	Four-wheel vented discs, 28.7 cm (11.3 in) diameter at front, 29.5 cm (11.6 in) diameter at rear
Body/chassis:	Steel square tube separate chassis with alloy and steel two-door coupé or convertible body

ITALY

133

ITALY

FERRARI DINO

The beautifully crafted and alluring Dino was Ferrari's first mid-engine road car, named by Enzo in tribute to his dead son, and never officially a Ferrari.

The Dino was the first mid-engined Ferrari, although with half the normal number of cylinders. The quad-cam V6 engine was shared with the front-engined Fiat Dino, and built by Fiat too. The unit found its way into the Fiat so that over 500 could be built to homologate the V6 for Formula Two racing.

On pre-1969 cars, the bodywork was alloy, although these 206GT cars had smaller engines. In 1969, the cars were given larger engines (now with an iron block), but to balance this out, the bodywork changed to steel. These heavier but more powerful Dinos were known as 246GTs.

Side vents provided additional cooling for the V6 engine, in addition to the front radiator.

134

The front trunk was useless for luggage, thanks to the spare wheel, battery and sharply angled radiator. However, because of the 'flying buttresses' at the rear, which meant the engine lid could be fitted quite far forward, there was another trunk behind it which was better.

The Ferrari badge on the rear was a later addition. Dinos were never badged as Ferraris.

nzo Ferrari's son, Alfredino, died of a kidney disease in 1957. Ferrari's founding father was heartbroken at the loss of his beloved son, and he never quite recovered.

Alfredino was remembered with the Dino 206GT, unveiled in 1967. A more glowing tribute could scarcely be imagined. Even though the Dino wasn't an official Ferrari – it was marketed as a separate marque – there was no mistaking the gorgeous Pininfarina body, superior handling and exceptional performance. It was pure Maranello magic through and through.

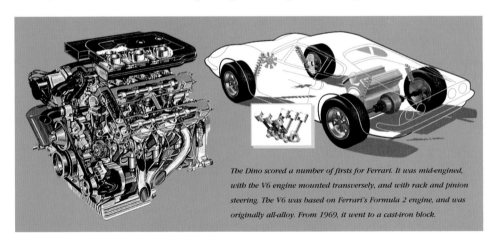

The Dino scored a number of firsts for Ferrari. It was mid-engined, with the V6 engine mounted transversely, and with rack and pinion steering. The V6 was based on Ferrari's Formula 2 engine, and was originally all-alloy. From 1969, it went to a cast-iron block.

Intended as a Porsche competitor, a prancing horse to battle the 911, the Dino was fitted with a smaller than normal V6 engine, and was mid-engined, the first road Ferrari to be so. In order to meet Formula Two racing regulations, over 500 production units had to be made. Such a number was beyond the small resources of Ferrari, but well within the capabilities of a large concern like Fiat. So Fiat made the engines, and also fitted them in its own Dino model.

Pininfarina worked wonders with the styling. It is one of the all-time classic masterpieces. The shape was so smooth and slippery that the car was capable of almost 242 km/h (150 mph).

Alloy, iron and steel

The early alloy engines were known to be rather fragile, so in 1969, a tougher iron block was used, and displacement upped to 2,418 cc (148 ci). These 246GTs had steel bodies, and a slightly longer wheelbase too.

In 1971, the 246GTS appeared, the S standing for Spyder. Its removable Targa roof panel made it a popular choice.

The Dino 246GT was replaced by the less aesthetically pleasing Dino 308GT4 in 1975.

Ferrari Dino

Top speed:	238 km/h (148 mph)
0-96 km/h (0-60 mph):	7.3 secs
Engine type:	V6
Displacement:	2,418 cc (148 ci)
Max power:	145 kW (195 bhp) @ 5,000 rpm
Max torque:	225 Nm (166 lb ft) @ 5,500 rpm
Weight:	1,187 kg (2,611 lb)
Economy:	7.8 km/l (22 mpg)
Transmission:	Five-speed manual
Brakes:	Four-wheel vented discs, 26.9 cm (10.6 in) in diameter
Body/chassis:	Tubular-steel chassis with steel two-door coupé body

ITALY

FERRARI 250 GT SWB

The name stands for Short Wheelbase Berlinetta, representing a classic racing and road thoroughbred, and one of the most exciting Ferraris ever created.

The rounded lines were, as with most Ferraris, created by Pininfarina. The body panels were hand-built in steel and alloy, although competition versions had their entire body made out of aluminium. Another weight-saving trick on the race cars was the use of plastic side windows.

The previous Testa Rossa, and the succeeding 250GTO came with a five-speed gearbox, but the SWB displayed its racing intentions by just being equipped with a four-speed transmission.

A range of different back axle ratios could be specified, resulting in top speeds between 201 km/h (125 mph) and a frightening 270 km/h (168 mph).

The all-alloy V12 engine was developed from an existing Ferrari engine, but with various modifications to make it easier to work on in race conditions, such as moving the spark plugs to make them more accessible for mechanics.

Disc brakes finally made an appearance on a Ferrari with the SWB. The vents underneath the headlamps (which didn't appear on road cars) were needed to cool the brakes. The vents in the wings behind each wheel served the same purpose.

The Ferrari 250GT range marked the start of volume road car production by Ferrari. Prior to 1954, Ferraris for the highway had been built in strictly limited numbers, but with the 250GT of 1954, manufacture suddenly went into the hundreds, almost reaching a thousand.

There were several more limited production models born out of the standard 250GT, but the most significant model – and the one which would become one of the most loved and admired Ferraris of all time – was the Ferrari 250GT SWB, first launched in 1959.

The all-alloy V12 included a number of refinements, such as all the spark plugs placed so race mechanics could get to them easily. It was a short stroke engine, which made it very fast revving. Three twin-choke carburettors were fitted as standard.

SW stood for short wheelbase, while B stood for Berlinetta, meaning 'little coupé' in Italian. The raison d'etre behind the SWB was that it could be a car just as good at racing as it was on the road. Ferrari wanted owners to drive it to the track, race it (and presumably win) and then drive it back home again.

Shortening the odds

Shortening the wheelbase of the standard 250GT stiffened the chassis up, and made the SWB very agile. Other advancements included all-round disc brakes, and a type 168 B V12 engine, offering considerable power. Pininfarina clothed most of the cars (there were some special-bodied versions though) with the beautiful body, built out of steel and aluminium by Scaglietti.

Two versions were launched at the 1959 Paris Motor Show, a racing GT version, and a Lusso model, for the road. Over the next few years, the SWB would go on to notch up some impressive victories in the hands of drivers like Stirling Moss.

In 1962, the SWB evolved into the lightweight 250GTO, probably the most celebrated Ferrari of all time.

Ferrari 250 GT SWB

Top speed:	225 km/h (140 mph)
0-96 km/h (0-60 mph):	6.7 secs
Engine type:	V12
Displacement:	2,953 cc (180 ci)
Max power:	209 kW (280 bhp) @ 7,000 rpm
Max torque:	275 Nm (203 lb ft) @ 5,500 rpm
Weight:	1,187 kg (2,611 lb)
Economy:	4.9 km/l (13.8 mpg)
Transmission:	Four-speed manual
Brakes:	Four-wheel discs
Body/chassis:	Tubular-steel ladder chassis with all-alloy or alloy and steel two-door coupé body

ITALY

141

FIAT 500

Fiat's baby 500 has become a cult car, a style icon far removed from its original concept as basic motorized transport for the Italian masses.

The 500 was the Italian version of the Mini, although it appeared two years before the British model. It was also shorter too. And, like the Mini and its Cooper derivative, sporty, tuned versions would appear, thanks to Abarth.

The rear swing axle suspension was very basic and made the Fiat's handling tricky on the limit. In extreme cases, the rear wheels could tuck in and cause the car to roll. This is a weakness of many rear-engined designs.

Pre-1965 cars had 'suicide' doors, hinged at the rear instead of the front. Estates kept them until 1977.

Sunroofs were a luxury on bigger cars, but standard on the 500, designed for hot climates. On convertible versions, the soft-top rolled right back to the engine lid, thanks to the plastic rear screen.

After Fiat had squeezed the spare tyre, battery and fuel tank into the front trunk, there wasn't much room for anything else.

The tiny engine had only two cylinders, but was all-aluminium. Power outputs were hardly impressive, up to 16 kW (22 bhp), but the engine could be tuned to produce more.

ITALY

143

I taly is often said to be one of the most stylish nations on Earth. Yet, usually, such style comes at a high price. Not so with the Fiat 500. The diminutive car, built from 1957 to 1977, has become a fashion statement, a minimalist luxury, but its original purpose was cheap and cheerful motoring for all.

The 500 Topolino, Fiat's original small economy car, had been around since pre-World War II days, when it was eventually replaced by the 500 Nuova. It was tiny, but

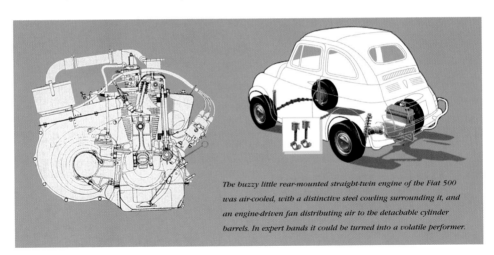

The buzzy little rear-mounted straight-twin engine of the Fiat 500 was air-cooled, with a distinctive steel cowling surrounding it, and an engine-driven fan distributing air to the detachable cylinder barrels. In expert hands it could be turned into a volatile performer.

undeniably cute, and its charm instantly won it many fans.

Despite the small engine, performance was lively, and the sometimes wayward handling certainly made it an exciting drive. Soon, 500s would be swarming all over Italian cities like motorized ants and, before long, would spread to other countries too. In total, four million would be made.

More power, more space

The engine was uprated in 1960, and the car became the 500D. A station wagon version – the Giardiniera – came the same year, with the novel innovation of the rear-mounted engine turned on its side under the floor.

1965 saw the 'suicide' doors replaced, with safer, but less interesting versions. Three years later, customers were treated to the 500L, with extra features and amenities such as a fuel gauge!

The final Nuova was the 500R of 1972, with the biggest engine yet seen on the car,

a 594 cc (36 ci) unit borrowed from another Fiat small car, the 126.

In 1975, sedan versions ended, although the Giardiniera, then built by Autobianchi, lasted a further two years. It was the end of the teddy bear on wheels.

Fiat 500

Top speed:	95 km/h (59 mph)
0-96 km/h (0-60 mph):	n/a
Engine type:	In-line twin
Displacement:	499 cc (30 ci)
Max power:	13 kW (18 bhp) @ 4,600 rpm
Max torque:	30 Nm (22 lb ft) @ 3,000 rpm
Weight:	471 kg (1,036 lb)
Economy:	16.3 km/l (46 mpg)
Transmission:	Four-speed manual
Brakes:	Four-wheel drums
Body/chassis:	Steel monocoque two-door sedan with fabric sunroof

ITALY

145

FORD GT40

When a company like Ford sets out on racing revenge, the result is bound to be spectacular. It led to the exciting and dramatic GT40.

A mid-engined layout was decided on to ensure racing competence. Power outputs from the small-block V8 varied from 228 kW (306 bhp) to a staggering 324 kW (435 bhp) in cars fitted with Gurney-Westlake cylinder heads.

Racers came with a four-speed transmission with the shifter mounted on the right. Road cars had a more conventional ZF five-speed box with the stick in the centre position.

The design of the GT40 was based on a Lola racing car, although enhanced at Ford's Dearborn studios. Because the body wasn't structural, it was made from fibreglass, all the strength coming from the chassis. Even the suspension uprights are made from magnesium to save weight.

The cramped, low cockpit of the GT40s wasn't designed for tall drivers, who would hit their heads on the gullwing doors. This car even has a streamlined bump added to the roof to increase interior height.

The radiator was mounted in the front, and cooled by air flowing through vents in the front hood.

Thick Halibrand wheels may look heavy, but magnesium rims kept the weight down. Knock-off spinners were used to make pit stops easier.

UNITED STATES

UNITED STATES

In 1963, Ford almost bought Ferrari. The deal floundered at the last moment when Enzo Ferrari discovered he wouldn't retain as much control over the company that bore his name as he had originally thought. Ford executives were apparently so incensed that they set out to get revenge by building a car capable of beating Ferrari at Le Mans.

The result was the GT40, one of the world's ultimate racers. The project was a collaboration between the US and the UK, with the cars being built in England at the Ford Advanced Vehicles plant near London. The cars were only 40 inches (101 cm) high, hence their name.

Choosing reliability over sophistication, most GT40s were fitted with highly tuneable

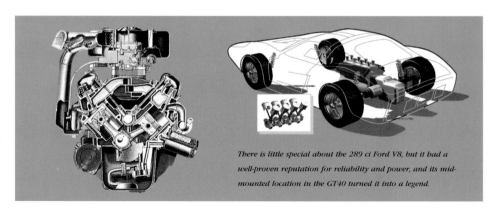

There is little special about the 289 ci Ford V8, but it had a well-proven reputation for reliability and power, and its mid-mounted location in the GT40 turned it into a legend.

V8 engines dating back to the 1950s, and similar to those used in Sunbeam Tigers, Ford Mustangs and AC Cobras.

In the 1964 Le Mans race, none of the GT40 cars finished. So Ford bought in Carroll Shelby to run the racing programme. Under his guidance, the Mk II GT40 appeared, with a seven-litre (427 ci) engine and a 322 km/h (200 mph) plus capability.

Victory at last

The changes paid off. In 1966, Ferrari was finally beaten at Le Mans when GT40s finished first, second and third.

After winning again in 1967, Ford withdrew from endurance racing with a packed trophy cabinet, although Mk III road versions of the GT40 continued to be built until 1969. However, privately entered GT40s wearing Gulf Oil colours scooped the Le Mans laurels again in 1968 and 1969. Revenge for Ford must have been very sweet indeed.

Ford GT40
(1967 Mk II road car)

Top speed:	265 km/h (165 mph)
0-96 km/h (0-60 mph):	5.5 secs
Engine type:	V8
Displacement:	4,735 cc (289 ci)
Max power:	228 kW (306 bhp) @ 6,000 rpm
Max torque:	444 Nm (328 lb ft) @ 4,200 rpm
Weight:	1,000 kg (2,200 lb)
Economy:	5.2 km/l (14.7 mpg)
Transmission:	Five-speed ZF manual transaxle
Brakes:	Four-wheel discs, 29.2 cm (11.5 in) diameter at front, 28.4 cm (11.2in) diameter at rear
Body/chassis:	Sheet steel central semi-monocoque with front and rear subframes and fibreglass two-door, two-seat GT body

UNITED STATES

Ford Model T

The cheap Model T was the first car to popularize motoring for the masses, but also enjoyed a second career as a hot-rod favourite.

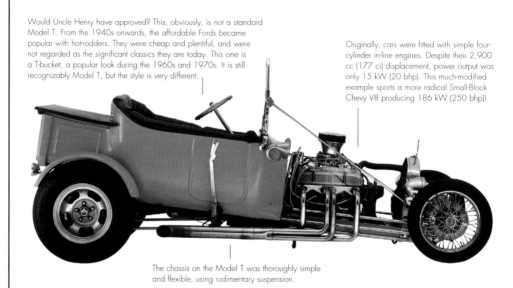

Would Uncle Henry have approved? This, obviously, is not a standard Model T. From the 1940s onwards, the affordable Fords became popular with hot-rodders. They were cheap and plentiful, and were not regarded as the significant classics they are today. This one is a T-bucket, a popular look during the 1960s and 1970s. It is still recognizably Model T, but the style is very different.

Originally, cars were fitted with simple four-cylinder in-line engines. Despite their 2,900 cc (177 ci) displacement, power output was only 15 kW (20 bhp). This much-modified example sports a more radical Small-Block Chevy V8 producing 186 kW (250 bhp)!

The chassis on the Model T was thoroughly simple and flexible, using rudimentary suspension.

Buttoned-leather was the usual interior trim in the majority of Model Ts.

The original Ford windscreen could be folded flat for extra ventilation.

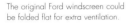

The original look of the Model T has been kept at the front, complete with the chrome Ford radiator grille. A nice touch on this example is the AA badge mounted on the radiator cap.

UNITED STATES

151

There is no point in anybody else explaining the thinking behind the Model T, when Henry Ford himself put it so eloquently: 'I will build a motor car for the great multitude ... constructed of the best materials, by the best men to be hired, after the simplest designs that modern engineering can devise... so low in price that no man making a good salary will be unable to own one, and enjoy with his family the blessing of hours of pleasure in God's great open spaces.'

The Model T is probably the most significant car of all time. It popularized the

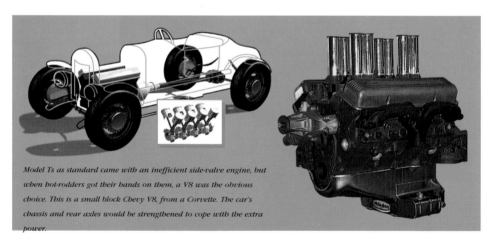

Model Ts as standard came with an inefficient side-valve engine, but when hot-rodders got their hands on them, a V8 was the obvious choice. This is a small block Chevy V8, from a Corvette. The car's chassis and rear axles would be strengthened to cope with the extra power.

idea of affordable motoring for everybody, by pioneering the use of mass production principles, transforming the auto industry by doing so. Affectionately known as the Tin Lizzie, its runaway success made its creator and his company incredibly rich and immensely powerful.

Low-cost ruggedness

The debut for the Model T was in 1908. It was a simple but robust machine, using lightweight vanadium steel in its frame to make it strong. Reliability wasn't good, but the car was so uncomplicated that it was cheap and easy to repair, and the cost of buying one fell yearly as more and more automation was introduced in its construction. When the car was first put on sale, it cost $825. By its final year, the price had dropped to just $290.

Across the world, 15,007,033 would be sold by the end of production in May 1927. By that time, sales were in free fall, the Model T then old-fashioned and unappealing compared to its rivals.

The sheer numbers available resulted in it enjoying a revival from the 1940s onwards, as a popular custom hot-rod base.

Ford Model T

Top speed:	71 km/h (44 mph)
0-96 km/h: (0-60 mph):	n/a
Engine type:	Side-valve four
Displacement:	2,890 cc (177 ci)
Max power:	15 kW (20 bhp) @ 1,800 rpm
Max torque:	111 Nm (82 lb ft) @ 900 rpm
Weight:	658 kg (1,450 lb)
Economy:	n/a
Transmission:	Two-speed epicyclic transmission
Brakes:	Two-wheel drums at rear
Body/chassis:	Simple separate steel chassis frame, with channel section side members, and cross bracing

UNITED STATES

Ford Mustang

The Ford Mustang was a runaway sales success, inventing the term 'pony car' as a description for the new breed of 1960s American sporty compacts.

The Mustang was available in hardtop, fastback and convertible forms. On the hardtop version, the side windows could be wound completely out of sight to create a pillarless look.

This is a Mustang GT 2 + 2 fastback, introduced in 1965. It came with a Challenger Special 289 V8 engine, front disc brakes, a three-speed manual transmission and extra gauges inside as standard.

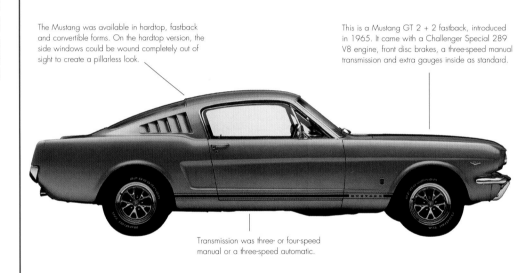

Transmission was three- or four-speed manual or a three-speed automatic.

The massive range of different options – part of the Ford 'Total Performance' programme – were made available for Mustang customers. Buyers could choose from suspension options, handling kits, interior packs, brake upgrades, power-assisted steering, air conditioning ... the list went on. With a Mustang to suit every taste, Ford sold a million cars within two years of its launch.

Mustangs were offered with either six-cylinder or V8 engines. The latter was by far the more popular option. The range of power outputs varied from a paltry 75 kW (101 bhp) to well over 317 kW (425 bhp).

UNITED STATES

155

The Ford Mustang owes its origins to another Blue Oval legend, the Thunderbird. When the T-Bird debuted, it was a racy two-seater, but it gradually grew larger. Ford vice-president Lee Iacocca was charged with the task of once again creating a fun 'personal car' for the 1960s. He managed this and much more besides: with the Mustang, Ford found itself with an icon to eclipse even the Thunderbird.

There had been prototype Mustangs before the official launch in April 1964, most prominently at the 1963 US Grand

Part of what made the Mustang range so attractive to buyers was the sheer range of options. Customers could specify straight-sixes or V8s, and this is just one of the latter, the very special high-compression Hi-Po 289.

Prix. The interest in it convinced Ford to build it as a commercial model.

The name summoned up images of the freedom and the pioneering spirit of the Wild West, just right for the image Ford was trying to project. It helped too that it was such a handsome-looking car, whether in notchback, fastback or convertible form, and was a thoroughly enjoyable car to drive.

What really sold the Mustang to the public was the vast amount of options that were available. Straight-six and V8 engines were available, and practically anything customers wanted to do to their new car, Ford were able to offer something to suit.

Pony car revolution

Other manufacturers rushed to build 'pony cars' to cash in on the Mustang's success, but few quite captured its spirit, especially after Carrol Shelby got his hands on a few, and created the awesome GT350 and GT500 Mustang models.

The Mustang started to grow longer, fatter and heavier from 1969, becoming less pretty as it did so. In 1973, it was restyled completely and its great looks disappeared.

Ford Mustang

Top speed:	204 km/h (123 mph)
0-96 km/h (0-60 mph):	7.3 secs
Engine type:	V8
Displacement:	4,735 cc (289 ci)
Max power:	202 kW (271 bhp) @ 6,000 rpm
Max torque:	421 Nm (312 lb ft) @ 3,400 rpm
Weight:	1,410 kg (3,100 lb)
Economy:	5.3 km/l (15 mpg)
Transmission:	Three-speed manual, four-speed manual or three-speed automatic
Brakes:	Discs at front, drums at rear
Body/chassis:	Subframe chassis construction with steel sedan, coupé and convertible bodies

UNITED STATES

FORD THUNDERBIRD

The Thunderbird was launched to combat arch-rival Chevrolet's new Corvette. Although it is still being built today, the original stylish two-seater lasted just three years.

A distinctive feature of the Thunderbird was the porthole window in the standard fibreglass hardtop. The top was bolt-on, but a folding soft-top could be specified.

The spare tyre was originally carried on the back of the car, above the bumper. This feature was dropped in 1957, when the trunk was redesigned so a tyre could be fitted inside.

Cooling flaps – known as 'crotch coolers' – were fitted because of poor ventilation, although how a convertible could have poor air circulation wasn't made clear.

The large chrome-grilled hood bulge cleared the air cleaners for the V8 engine and looked cool, too.

Following the American trend, tail fins made an appearance in 1957, although they would never scale the monstrous heights of many other US cars available at the time.

Before the corrosive qualities of exhaust fumes were fully understood, siting the pipes in the chrome fenders was a popular design detail of many 1950s cars. This soon changed, once the metalwork around the exhausts started to disappear.

UNITED STATES

159

After World War II, a wave of sporty European imports started to flood into the United States. Chevrolet was the first homegrown manufacturer to fight back, introducing the two-seater, fibreglass Corvette in 1953.

If Ford was slow in reacting to European competitors, it certainly was not going to let Chevy steal the glory for long. A year later came the Thunderbird. Like the Corvette, it was a racy two-seater and an elegant and attractive convertible. Unlike the Chevy, though, it had the powerful V8 engine right from the start.

American myth

The Thunderbird was not quite in the Corvette mould. With heavier and softer

What other choice could there be for a sporty Ford than a V8? The conventional unit was designed more for cruising than speed, but with the addition of a Paxton-McCulloch supercharger, power shot up to 224 kW (300 bhp).

handling, Ford billed it more as a 'personal luxury car', but it still outsold the 'Vette right from the start. It also became the stuff of popular folklore too. Songs were written featuring the car, it appeared in films, and stars drove them in real life: Marilyn Monroe bought her Sunset Coral one in 1956.

Powered initially by a 4,785 cc (292 ci) V8, size went up to 5,112 cc (312 ci) after a year, and there were minor cosmetic changes. There were more obvious alterations for 1957, with fins added, the hood extended and a different frontal arrangement. A highly desirable F-Bird became available. With a supercharger fitted, it pumped out an enormous 254 kW (340 bhp) against the standard version's 201 kW (270 bhp).

There was a radical makeover for 1958. Extra seats were added to make a four-seater, and lots of chrome detailing was added. It was not at all the car it had started out as just a few years before. The T-Bird

legend would continue ... but it just would not be quite as epic as it had been.

Ford Thunderbird

Top speed:	196 km/h (122 mph)
0-96 km/h (0-60 mph):	9.5 secs
Engine type:	V8
Displacement:	4,785 cc (292 ci)
Max power:	158 kW (212 bhp) @ 4,400 rpm
Max torque:	402 Nm (297 lb ft) @ 2,700 rpm
Weight:	1,386 kg (3,050 lb)
Economy:	4.6 km/l (13 mpg)
Transmission:	Three-speed manual with optional overdrive, or three-speed automatic
Brakes:	Four-wheel drums, with optional power assistance
Body/chassis:	Separate cruciform steel chassis with steel two-door body. Choice of removable hardtop or convertible roof

UNITED STATES

JAGUAR E-TYPE

The Jaguar E-type is a worthy candidate for title of most beautiful car ever built. Over 40 years after its launch, it still looks stunning.

The most desirable body style was the convertible, but the E-type also came as a coupé and 2+2.

The long and low hood was a major contribution to the E-type's sleek looks. 14 louvres on the bonnet allowed heat to escape from the hardworking engine. The hood hinged forward, allowing good access to work on the mechanics.

The XK engine used in the E-type appeared in original form in 1948. In 1971, Jaguar fitted its new V12 engine to try and prolong the life of the aging sports car. A bigger grille was fitted on these Series III cars to improve the cooling for this larger engine.

Early E-types had faired-in headlamps. In 1967, these were altered to exposed light units to meet US Federal regulations.

Three windscreen wipers were necessary to keep the windshield clean, although the Series III car managed to make do with just two.

The E-type was the first Jaguar to boast independent rear suspension. Mounted on its own separate subframe, it can be removed completely from the car without dismantling. Front suspension was a well-proven double wishbone arrangement.

UNITED KINGDOM

The E-type was one of the most iconic sports cars of all time. It rewrote the rules on how to build a 241 km/h (150 mph) supercar and amazed the world when it debuted in 1961. Performance motoring would never be the same again.

Jaguar's masterpiece was developed from the racing D-type of the 1950s. The tried and tested XK 3,781 cc (230 ci) six-cylinder engine was mated with new all-independent suspension and a sublimely beautiful and sleek body to produce a car that cost less

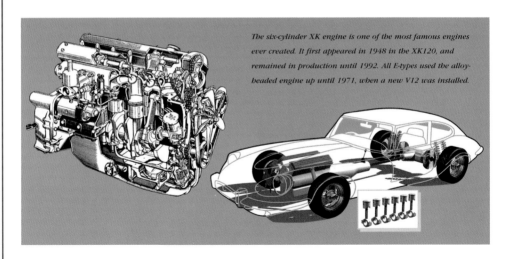

The six-cylinder XK engine is one of the most famous engines ever created. It first appeared in 1948 in the XK120, and remained in production until 1992. All E-types used the alloy-beaded engine up until 1971, when a new V12 was installed.

than half of a comparable Aston Martin or Ferrari. In tests, it managed to top 241 km/h (150 mph), and although production cars fell a little short of this magic figure, E-types were still sublime to look at and equally sublime to drive.

The cat develops

Available as a coupé and convertible, a more torquey 4,235 cc (258 ci) engine arrived in 1964, and a longer 2+2 version joined the range in 1966. US federal regulations dictated bigger bumpers and uncowled headlamps on the Series II of 1968, which compromised some of the original design purity. In 1971, the Series III redefined the E-type concept as almost a muscle car, squeezing Jaguar's brutal V12 engine under the bonnet, and giving the leaping cat a prominent front grille, fatter wheels and flared wheel arches.

This proved to be the last design and mechanical update for the legend. Within four years, the E-type would be dropped from production. Yet even today, the car remains the superlative by which all other sports cars are judged.

Jaguar E-type

Top speed:	241 km/h (150 mph)
0-96 km/h (0-60 mph):	7.3 secs
Engine type:	In-line six
Displacement:	3,781 cc (230 ci)
Max power:	198 kW (265 bhp) @ 5,500 rpm
Max torque:	352 Nm (260 lb ft) @ 4,000 rpm
Weight:	1,120 kg (2,463 lb)
Economy:	5.1 km/l (14.5 mpg)
Transmission:	Four-speed manual
Brakes:	Four-wheel discs, inboard at rear
Body/chassis:	Steel body with centre steel monocoque chassis and front and rear subframes

UNITED KINGDOM

JAGUAR MK 2

The definitive Jaguar sedan of the 1960s era, the curvaceous Mk 2 was also one of the British firm's most attractively styled and enduring classics.

The interior was up to Jaguar's normal standards. Upholstery was (initially) leather, with deep-pile carpeting, a wooden dashboard, door cappings and rear picnic tables. From 1966, cheaper Ambla plastic upholstery came instead of hide.

The trusty old XK engine, in 2.4-, 3.4- and 3.8-litre (146, 207 and 232 ci) sizes, could be found under the hood. However, the Daimler version had a smooth V8 unit.

The Mk 2 became the Jaguar 240/340 in 1967. Visually, although the shape remained the same, slimmer bumpers were fitted and the front auxiliary driving lamps were replaced by dummy chrome grilles.

The Mk 2 was, logically, a development of the Mk 1, but was a prettier design than its predecessor, with slimmer roof pillars and better-balanced proportions. It was flashier too, with extra glass and chrome.

In 1962, a Daimler-badged version of the Mk 2 joined the line-up. As well as a different engine, it could be distinguished by a 'D' insignia on the front, and a fluted front grille and rear trunk handle.

UNITED KINGDOM

167

Jaguar's first mid-sized luxury car was the Mk 1 of 1955. Despite slightly awkward styling, it proved a fruitful design exercise.

In 1959 came a major revamp by Jaguar boss William Lyons. The somewhat dumpy lines of the Mk 1 were transformed into an elegant and smooth sedan, with gorgeous curvaceous styling that would help establish Jaguar as one of Britain's foremost luxury car manufacturers of the era. The interior of the car was a palace of indulgence

There were three six-cylinder twin overhead-camshaft XK engine options for the Mk 2: 2.4 (2,483 cc/152 ci), 3.4 (3,424 cc/209 ci) or 3.8 (3,781 cc/231 ci). The latter was the star performer and is regarded among enthusiasts as one of the truly classic Jaguar creations. On the Mk 2, it was fitted with twin SU carburettors.

with wood, hide and deep-pile carpeting providing a memorable driving experience.

The Mk 2 was available as a 2.4-, 3.4- or 3.8-litre (146, 207 and 232 ci) model. The latter was the flagship, the powerful 164 kW (220 bhp) XK six-cylinder engine making it the fastest European sedan available on the market. It was also popular with criminals who viewed it as the perfect getaway vehicle. The British police had to buy their own Mk 2s just to keep up.

Same style, new names

The shape was used for a Daimler version in 1962, using that firm's old V8 engine. The extra two cylinders gave smoother delivery, but the car was slower than the Mk 2 3.4- or 3.8-litre models. But that did not matter to the older generation at whom the Daimler was marketed.

Forced to start saving money in 1966, Jaguar downgraded the specification of the Mk 2 a year later, the cars were renamed as Jaguar 240s and 340s, with even more cost-cutting.

The models were discontinued in 1969, but echoes of the styling live on in Jaguar's current S-type.

Jaguar Mk 2

Top speed:	201 km/h (125 mph)
0-96 km/h: (0-60 mph):	9.2 secs
Engine type:	In-line six
Displacement:	3,781 cc (231 ci)
Max power:	164 kW (220 bhp) @ 5,500 rpm
Max torque:	325 Nm (240 lb ft) @ 3,000 rpm
Weight:	1,545 kg (3,400 lb)
Economy:	7.4 km/l (21 mpg)
Transmission:	Four-speed manual with overdrive or three-speed automatic
Brakes:	Four-wheel discs
Body/chassis:	Unitized chassis with steel four-door sedan body

UNITED KINGDOM

LAMBORGHINI COUNTACH

From any angle, the Lamborghini Countach was a spectacular piece of design. But it did not just look good – performance was just as dramatic as the styling.

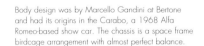

Body design was by Marcello Gandini at Bertone and had its origins in the Carabo, a 1968 Alfa Romeo-based show car. The chassis is a space frame birdcage arrangement with almost perfect balance.

As if the rest of the car wasn't already sensational, the doors were one of the most notable elements of the Countach's design. They pivoted upwards when opened, and were held in place by a gas strut.

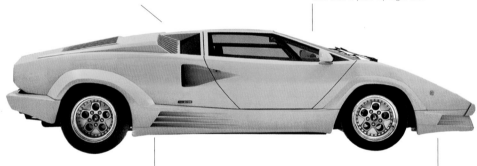

The V12 engine was mid-mounted, and cooled by the large ducts behind the doors, as well as electric fans.

The short nose of the Countach means there's not much room for luggage. There is another trunk at the rear.

Don't look for rust on the body of a Countach. All of it is alloy, except for the doors, which are made of fibreglass.

A conspicuous rear spoiler was an optional extra, useful for providing extra downforce. And it looked good too.

Flared wheel arches appeared with the LP400S of 1978, to accommodate larger wheels and tyres. Before this change, the car had a trapezoidal wheel arch shape at the rear.

ITALY

How do you follow a car like the Miura? Building a successor to the first mid-engined supercar was never going to be easy for Lamborghini, but it rose to the challenge magnificently with the radical Countach.

Company founder Ferruccio Lamborghini had been a tractor manufacturer, who entered sports car production only after an argument with Enzo Ferrari. Trying to beat its Italian rival would be the constant theme of Lamborghini's cars. Although the prancing horse would always have its impassioned admirers, in many ways, Lamborghinis were much more impressive and radical.

The Miura was a case in point, beating Ferrari to the accolade of the first manufacturer to build a mid-engined

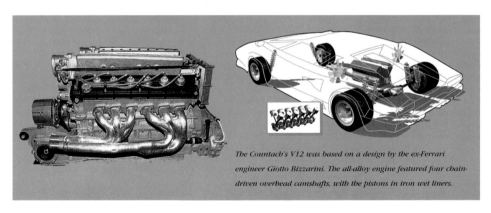

The Countach's V12 was based on a design by the ex-Ferrari engineer Giotto Bizzarini. The all-alloy engine featured four chain-driven overhead camshafts, with the pistons in iron wet liners.

production supercar. But Lamborghini wasn't content to rest on its laurels. It knew it had to come up with something extraordinary to perpetuate its legend...

The Countach was just the thing. The razor-sharp, angular body was outlandish for its era, when curves were still the norm. It was penned by Marcello Gandini at Bertone, who had also come up with the Miura. As before, the four-litre (244 ci) engine was mid-mounted for great handling.

Ferrari beater

The first series was known as the LP400, and was supplanted in 1978 by the LP400S, with body flaring and a much meaner look. The engine was taken up to 4.8 litres (293 ci) in 1982 with the LP500S, again to battle Ferrari and its new Boxer.

Ferrari responded with the Testarossa in 1985, so Lamborghini hit back with a smoother-looking Countach, known as the Quattrovalvole, with 339 kW (455 bhp).

After a production run of 20 years, the Countach was replaced by the equally astonishing Diablo in 1991.

Lamborghini Countach

Top speed:	286 km/h (178 mph)
0-96 km/h (0-60 mph):	5.2 secs
Engine type:	V12
Displacement:	5,167 cc (315 ci)
Max power:	339 kW (455 bhp) @ 7,000 rpm
Max torque:	500 Nm (369 lb ft) @ 5,200 rpm
Weight:	1,449 kg (3,188 lb)
Economy:	4.2 km/l (11.8 mpg)
Transmission:	Five-speed manual
Brakes:	Four-wheel vented discs, 30.0 cm (11.8 in) diameter at front, 27.9 cm (11 in) diameter at rear
Body/chassis:	Tubular-steel space-frame chassis with alloy and fibreglass two-door, two-seat body.

ITALY

LAMBORGHINI MIURA

Lamborghini had only been building sports cars for three years when it unveiled the innovative and spectacular mid-engined Miura and changed the world of supercars.

The V12 engine had four camshafts and was designed by Giotto Bizzarini, the man who had led the development on the Ferrari 250 GTO. It was mounted transversely just behind the cockpit, to make the Miura very compact.

Surprisingly for a supercar, the body was steel, but some concessions were made to weight-saving by having the hood and front section of the bodywork in alloy.

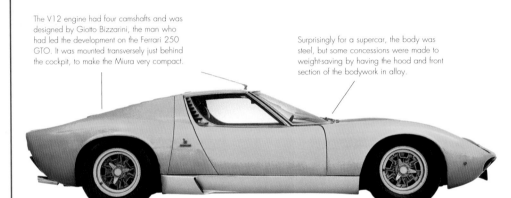

The cooling vents for the engine bay were mounted into the doors. The door handles actually formed part of the cooling fins.

The lights folded back into the bodywork when not in use. The lamp units were shared with the less glamorous Fiat 850, but were given extra appeal by the 'eyebrow' vents above and below them. The vents are purely cosmetic though.

Rear visibility was appalling. Slats were fitted over the engine to vent the heat from the engine compartment, and did a fine job of obscuring the view from the rear window as well.

The front contained the spare tyre and slanted radiator. There wasn't much room for anything else.

Enzo Ferrari was famous for his ability to upset people. The Italian genius may have been responsible for some wonderful cars, but his social graces left much to be desired.

In the early 1960s, he managed to offend Ferruccio Lamborghini, a wealthy agricultural machinery manufacturer. When Lamborghini complained about one of his Ferraris, he was told the fault was with him, not the car. He was just a tractor maker, who didn't understand real engineering, and was lucky to be able to buy a Ferrari at all.

Lamborghini decided to get his own back in an unusual way. He set himself up as a car manufacturer, determined to teach Ferrari a

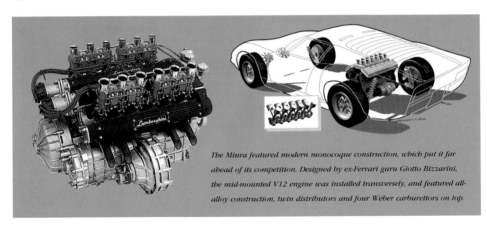

The Miura featured modern monocoque construction, which put it far ahead of its competition. Designed by ex-Ferrari guru Giotto Bizzarini, the mid-mounted V12 engine was installed transversely, and featured all-alloy construction, twin distributors and four Weber carburettors on top.

little about respect and a lot about building supercars. His first car was the 350GT of 1963. Then, in 1966, came the glorious Miura.

The Miura was named after a breed of fighting bull. It lived up to its aggressive name and was capable of beating anything coming from Ferrari. The svelte body came from Bertone's Marcello Gandini. Incredibly, it was his first design.

Clever engine thinking

Chief innovation was the V12 engine mounted transversely in the middle of the car. It took its inspiration from racing, but made the technology available for road use. Chief influence was Ford's GT40, but the idea to turn the engine sideways came from another source – the Mini! This approach meant the Miura was a very compact package, which promoted excellent balance and handling.

The Miura was also known as the TP400, and was joined in 1970 by the more highly tuned TP400S version. A year later came the furious 287 kW (385 bhp) TP400SV, of which just 150 were made.

Lamborghini Miura (TP400S)

Top speed:	277 km/h (172 mph)
0-96 km/h (0-60 mph):	6.9 secs
Engine type:	V12
Displacement:	3,929 cc (240 ci)
Max power:	496 kW (370 bhp) @ 7,700 rpm
Max torque:	388 Nm (286 lb ft) @ 5,500 rpm
Weight:	1,296 kg (2,851 lb)
Economy:	4 km/l (11.2 mpg)
Transmission:	Five-speed manual
Brakes:	Four-wheel solid discs, 30.0 cm (11.8 in) diameter at front, 30.7 cm (12.1 in) diameter at rear
Body/chassis:	Steel monocoque platform with steel and alloy two-door, two-seat coupé body

ITALY

177

LANCIA DELTA INTEGRALE

Like the Stratos before it, the Lancia Delta Integrale was a rally track special, which just happened to make a charismatic road car as well.

The Integrale used the modified bodyshell of the mundane Delta, first seen in 1979. Group A rally regulations dictated that competition cars had to bear at least a superficial resemblance to road cars.

The two-litre (122 ci) engine was originally used in the Lancia Thema sedan. However, multipoint fuel injection, electronic ignition and a Garrett T3 turbocharger boosted power considerably over its humbler stablemate. Final versions produced 160 kW (215 bhp).

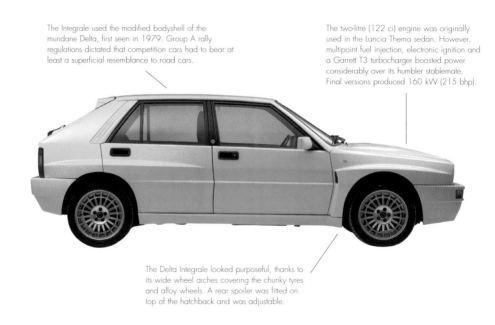

The Delta Integrale looked purposeful, thanks to its wide wheel arches covering the chunky tyres and alloy wheels. A rear spoiler was fitted on top of the hatchback and was adjustable.

Extra cooling vents were cut into the bonnet to provide fresh air to the hot engine.

The Delta Integrale handled superbly thanks to its permanent four-wheel drive system. It featured an epicyclic centre differential with viscous coupling and a Torsen unit at the rear. 47 per cent of the torque goes to the front wheels, 53 per cent goes to the rear.

Although sold in right-hand drive markets, the Integrale was only available with its steering wheel on the left.

ITALY

Lancia had dominated rallying during the mid-1970s with the Stratos. By the mid-1980s, it was back, and once more eager to win as many laurels as it could.

The Delta was originally available as a front-wheel drive box-like family hatchback, with a 1,995 cc (122 ci) engine. It fulfilled a need, but was hardly notable, although the Italian firm had entered an extreme mid-engined Delta four-wheel drive rally car in Group B rallies in 1984–85. Such cars were banned after some serious accidents, so Lancia turned its attention to the less demanding Group A instead.

In 1986 came the Delta HF 4 x 4, which managed to win the World Championship

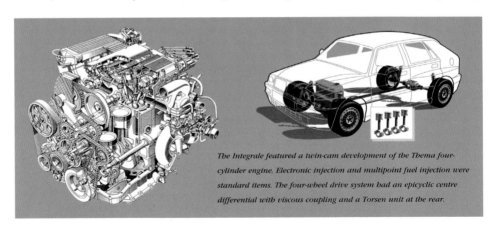

The Integrale featured a twin-cam development of the Thema four-cylinder engine. Electronic injection and multipoint fuel injection were standard items. The four-wheel drive system had an epicyclic centre differential with viscous coupling and a Torsen unit at the rear.

in 1987. That was not enough for Lancia though, and in October 1987 came the Delta Integrale, the word meaning 'complete' in Italian. And the Integrale was a complete performer. Despite its blocky, unaerodynamic looks, it had electrifying handling, and a top speed approaching 241 km/h (150 mph). All this from a car which still looked like the humble hatchback which sired it, albeit a more muscular version with a body kit and big wheel arches.

Evoluzione evolution

For 1990, there was a 16-valve version, and in 1991 came the Integrale Evoluzione, with more power, a better suspension set up and a tailgate spoiler to improve stability. An Evoluzione 2 appeared for 1992.

Integrale owners could take great pride in the fact that they were driving the same basic version of the car which won the World Rally Championship for Makes every year from 1987 to 1992, even if sometimes its suspect build quality did occasionally disappoint.

The Integrale departed in 1994, leaving a void which has yet to be filled.

Lancia Delta Integrale

Top speed:	220 km/h (137 mph)
0-96 km/h (0-60 mph):	5.7 secs
Engine type:	In-line four
Displacement:	1,995 cc (122 ci)
Max power:	157 kW (210 bhp) @ 5,750 rpm
Max torque:	308 Nm (227 lb ft) @ 2,500 rpm
Weight:	1,343 kg (2,954 lb)
Economy:	7.8 km/l (22 mpg)
Transmission:	Five-speed manual
Brakes:	Vented discs, 27.9 cm (11 in) diameter at front, solid discs, 25.4 cm (10 in) diameter at rear
Body/chassis:	Steel monocoque five-door hatchback

ITALY

LANCIA STRATOS

Lancia constructed the enigmatic Stratos solely to win the World Rally Championship. The production road cars were an afterthought, built just to satisfy homologation rules.

ITALY

Lancia was owned by Fiat, who also owned Ferrari by this time. That gave Lancia access to Ferrari technology and resulted in the use of a Dino V6 quad-cam engine for the Stratos. As was accepted racing practice, it was mid-mounted.

All panels on the Stratos were lightweight fibreglass. Both front and rear sections could be lifted off, a vital consideration for maintenance during a rally. They were held down by straps.

Design was by Bertone, and heavily based on two concept cars – also called the Stratos – which had appeared at the 1970 and 1971 Turin Motor Shows. The wedge shape was starting to become very fashionable and made the Stratos very aerodynamic. The bodies and chassis were also built by Bertone, then sent to Lancia for running gear to be added.

The central spoiler had three uses. Its conventional purpose was to provide extra downforce, but it also channelled air into the engine ducts and acted as a roll-over bar in the event of an accident.

Underneath the pointed nose was a radiator, two cooling fans and the spare tyre.

ITALY

183

A Stratos does not make a good road car. The cabin is noisy, cramped, uncomfortable and hot. It is a beast to drive, with poor rear visibility, erratic handling and perilous oversteer. The V6 engine makes it incredibly powerful, but taxing to pilot at ordinary speeds. And there is not a chance that there is any room for shopping, either.

But Lancia did not build the Stratos for the road. It was a pure-bred rally car, something it was very successful at. The fact that it would turn into a highly individual road coupé was just a lucky bonus.

The Stratos iron block/alloy head V6 engine had an illustrious and proven heritage, having been previously used in the Ferrari and Fiat Dinos. There were four chain-driven overhead camshafts, with three downdraft twin-choke Weber carburettors to spoon the fuel in. As with the Ferrari, it was mid-mounted in the Stratos.

Bertone concept, Dino power

The birth of the Stratos was brought about by the imminent demise of the Fulvia. The latter had had a prosperous rally career, but there was no obvious successor. Then, in November 1970, Lancia's competition director Cesare Fiorio saw a Bertone concept car at the Turin Motor Show. The wedge-shaped, low-slung futuristic design was not an obvious rally contender, but Fiorio was still inspired by what he saw. In 1971, a restyled version appeared, this time taller and powered by a Ferrari Dino V6 engine. Fiorio knew that he now had his next rally car.

There was a need to build 500 road cars for homologation – and in a hurry. The rally Stratos won its first event in April 1973, and then went on to dominate rallying, taking the World Championship in 1974, 1975 and 1976. It needed a skilled driver to wrest the best from it, but it could beat anything in the right hands.

The Stratos was only built from 1973 to 1975 but some of the road cars could still be bought 'new' up until 1980.

Lancia Stratos (road car version)

Top speed:	225 km/h (140 mph)
0-96 km/h (0-60 mph):	7.0 secs
Engine type:	V6
Displacement:	2,418 cc (148 ci)
Max power:	142 kW (190 bhp) @ 7,000 rpm
Max torque:	225 Nm (166 lb ft) @ 5,500 rpm
Weight:	982 kg (2,161 lb)
Economy:	6 km/l (17 mpg)
Transmission:	Five-speed manual
Brakes:	Four-wheel vented discs, 25.1 cm (9.9 in) diameter
Body/chassis:	Fibreglass two-door, two-seat coupé body with folded sheet-steel frame

ITALY

185

LAND ROVER SERIES I

The practical Land Rover was an accidental success, a stop-gap, basic and austere Jeep lookalike which became a surprise legend with a long production life.

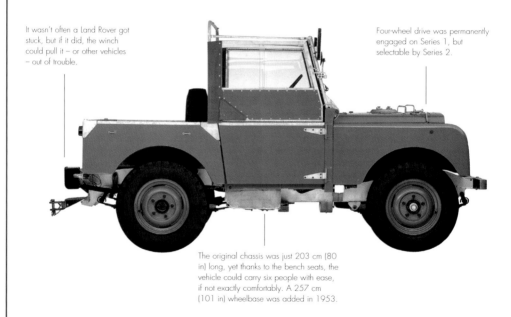

It wasn't often a Land Rover got stuck, but if it did, the winch could pull it – or other vehicles – out of trouble.

Four-wheel drive was permanently engaged on Series 1, but selectable by Series 2.

The original chassis was just 203 cm (80 in) long, yet thanks to the bench seats, the vehicle could carry six people with ease, if not exactly comfortably. A 257 cm (101 in) wheelbase was added in 1953.

Initial plans for the Land Rover envisaged a steering wheel in the centre, to keep export costs down. It was dropped because it wasn't practical. Other shelved money-saving schemes included having doors, a roof, a spare tyre and a passenger seat as extras!

Two body styles were originally offered. By far the most popular was the pickup, with a canvas roof. A more stylish station wagon was also available, but didn't sell as well.

You could have a Land Rover in any colour, so long as it was green. In 1954, blue and grey were added as colour schemes.

The simple and cheap steel box-frame chassis was Jeep-inspired and was very rugged.

L ife was tough and austere immediately after World War II. Throughout Europe, there were severe shortages of everything, and as a result, many ex-military vehicles found their way into civilian hands.

Maurice Wilks, Rover's chief engineer, bought a Willys Jeep and was impressed by it. Why not, he reasoned, build a British version as a temporary measure to bring in cash? It could even be built largely out of aluminium to get around steel shortages.

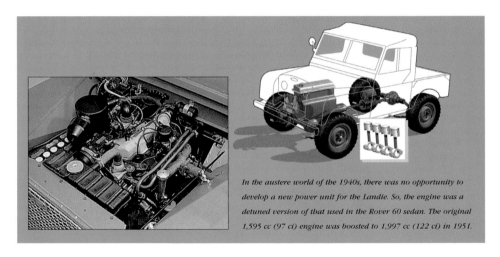

In the austere world of the 1940s, there was no opportunity to develop a new power unit for the Landie. So, the engine was a detuned version of that used in the Rover 60 sedan. The original 1,595 cc (97 ci) engine was boosted to 1,997 cc (122 ci) in 1951.

It took just a year to design and produce the Land Rover. The body was primitive – simple alloy panels were mounted on a box-section chassis. As many standard car parts as possible were incorporated to keep costs down, including the petrol engine and gearbox which came from the P3 sedan. It wasn't the sort of vehicle which should have excited anybody.

Surprise success

So Rover was surprised but delighted when it did. The Land Rover received a rapturous reception when launched at the 1948 Amsterdam Motor Show. The media and public alike loved the practical go anywhere vehicle. Orders from all over the world started to flood in. Soon, Rover were building more off-roaders than cars.

The 'Landie' was gradually improved. The headlamps were moved to the bumpers in 1951, and the engine grew larger. A longer wheelbase became available in 1953.

In 1958, the original model was superseded by the improved Series II, but the name – and concept – still lives on today with the Defender.

Land Rover Series 1

Top speed:	96.5 km/h (60 mph)
0-96 km/h (0-60 mph):	n/a
Engine type:	In-line four
Displacement:	1,997 cc (122 ci)
Max power:	38 kW (52 bhp) @ 4,000 rpm
Max torque:	137 Nm (101 lb ft) @ 1,500 rpm
Weight:	1,349 kg (2,968 lb)
Economy:	6.2 km/l (17.5 mpg)
Transmission:	Four-speed manual with two-speed transfer box
Brakes:	Four-wheel drums
Body/chassis:	Separate chassis with aluminium two-door open body

UNITED KINGDOM

LINCOLN CONTINENTAL

The choice of American presidents, the 1961–1969 Lincoln range was hugely imposing yet dignified and restrained, projecting an air of American solidity to the world.

Lincoln's luxury highway hauler was initially only available as a hardtop sedan or a four-door convertible. When the latter was launched in 1961, Lincoln was the only US manufacturer to build an open four-door car.

The Lincoln Continental was not the fastest American car, but it did boast the biggest engine. The 7,046 cc (430 ci) V8 grew to 7,571 cc (462 ci) in 1966. The emphasis was on torque, rather than power output.

Few cars had 'suicide' doors by the 1960s, but they made the Continental easy to enter and exit.

The clean, balanced lines of the 1961
to 1969 Continentals were styled by
Elwood Engel, and were a complete
contrast to the previous Continental series,
which was over-ornamented and fussy.

Because of the type of customers the Continental
was sold to, stringent quality control was paramount.
Engines were tested for three hours at almost
maximum revs, and then thoroughly inspected.
Checks were made on almost 200 components, and
every day a car was pulled from the production line
to check for tolerances. Finally, every Continental
was given a 19 km (12 mile) road test.

Much of the Lincoln Continental's worldwide fame comes from a particularly tragic chapter in American history. It was in a stretched Presidential 1961 Continental that John F Kennedy was assassinated in Dallas in 1963. The event marked the Lincoln out for

immortality, destined to appear in repeated grainy cine film and newsreel footage for decades to come.

The Continental name – in the US at least – first appeared on a styling exercise by Edsel Ford. He had been on a trip across America and wanted to make a car that

The Continental was the flagship Ford in the 1960s, and therefore had the Blue Oval's biggest and best engine. The 7,046 cc (430 ci) V8 was detuned to make it smoother, reduce the noise and improve fuel consumption.

symbolized what the continent meant to him. Public response to the vehicle resulted in it being put into production in 1941.

The name was revived in the mid-1950s as a Cadillac Eldorado beater. And as with the Eldorado, the Continental grew more garish as the decade progressed, sprouting vast amounts of lavish chrome and metal work

Fresh 1960s appeal

So the 1961 reincarnation of the Continental was a refreshing surprise. Gone were all of the extremes which had characterized the previous series, replaced by one of the most influential designs of the era. It was dignified-looking, combining a domineering attitude with a lot of class – the perfect statesman's choice.

To emphasize the point that the Continental was the best American car money could buy, Lincoln fitted it with the largest V8 available from Detroit and increased the options list as well. If there

was a feature that could be power-operated, then Lincoln would offer it.

The look of the 1961 Continental was so advanced that the basic shape stayed the same until 1969, with an even bigger V8 engine making an appearance in 1968.

Lincoln Continental

Top speed:	188 km/h (117 mph)
0-96 km/h (0-60mph):	11.2 secs
Engine type:	V8
Displacement:	7,046 cc (430 ci)
Max power:	224 kW (300 bhp) @ 4,100 rpm
Max torque:	630 Nm (465 lb ft) @ 2,000 rpm
Weight:	2,372 kg (5,220 lb)
Economy:	4.3 km/l (12 mpg)
Transmission:	Turbo-drive three-speed automatic
Brakes:	Four-wheel drums
Body/chassis:	Separate chassis with steel four-door sedan or convertible body

UNITED STATES

LOTUS ELAN

The Elan was not just among the prettiest sports cars of its day. It was – and still is – one of the best-handling cars money could buy.

Many of the Elan Sprint models featured an attractive two-tone colour scheme, divided by a contrasting border line.

Engines were based on Ford's Kent unit, used in the Anglia and Cortina, among others. However, a twin-cam head and twin carburettors gave much better performance than the standard Ford item. The same engines would also be fitted to Lotus Cortinas. Later Sprints featured a powerful 'Big Valve' version.

A lightweight fibreglass body was another Elan ingenuity, Lotus being a pioneer in this field. It was fitted to a strong steel backbone chassis, which endowed the Elan with much of its legendary handling capabilities.

Pop-up headlamps were novel on a British car of this era, especially one intended as a 'budget' sports car. They were designed to meet American headlight height regulations, and were operated by a vacuum system.

The Elan was the world's first production car to feature body-moulded bumpers, an innovation by designer Ron Hickman. They were based on his ideas for a Ford Anglia sports car which never materialized.

195

As impressive and daring as the Lotus Elite (1957 to 1963) may have been, it didn't do much good for the financial situation at Lotus. In the early 1960s, the company found itself on the verge of bankruptcy and boss Colin Chapman badly needed a profitable model.

Not even he could have foreseen the immense success of the Elan though. It is fair to say that the Elan made Lotus as a car manufacturer, earning it a road reputation to match its considerable racing fame. Even today, an Elan's road manners still impress; back in the 1960s, they were a revelation.

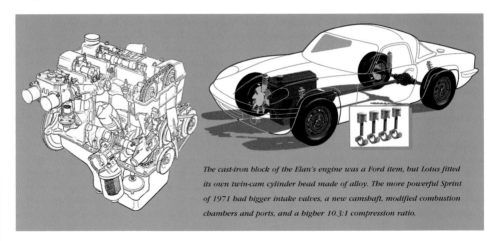

The cast-iron block of the Elan's engine was a Ford item, but Lotus fitted its own twin-cam cylinder head made of alloy. The more powerful Sprint of 1971 had bigger intake valves, a new camshaft, modified combustion chambers and ports, and a higher 10.3:1 compression ratio.

An added bonus was that the car looked so good as well.

The man behind the Elan was Ron Hickman, who had been a stylist at Ford. He had come up with an idea for an Anglia-based two-seater, but it never made it into production. Joining Lotus in 1958 gave him the chance to put his ideas into operation.

The secret of the Elan's success was its pressed-steel backbone chassis, race-bred suspension and lightweight fibreglass body, while retractable headlamps and body-moulded bumpers were novel features. Plus there was the twin-cam engine providing a high level of performance.

Elan evolution

The two-seater Elan – available in coupé and hardtop form – developed over several series. The S2 of 1964 had better brakes and an enhanced interior, the S3 of 1965 had a final higher drive, and in 1968, the S4 added flared wheel arches. The longer four-seater

Elan + 2 joined the range in 1967. But it would be 1971 Elan Sprint, with its dynamic 'Big Valve' engine which would become the ultimate model, capable of 200 km/h (124 mph) and finished in two-tone paintwork. Production finished in 1973.

Lotus Elan

Top speed:	190 km/h (118 mph)
0-96 km/h (0-60mph):	7.0 secs
Engine type:	In-line four
Displacement:	1,558 cc (95 ci)
Max power:	94 kW (126 bhp) @ 6,500 rpm
Max torque:	153 Nm (113 lb ft) @ 5,500 rpm
Weight:	687 kg (1,515 lb)
Economy:	9.2 km/l (26 mpg)
Transmission:	Four-speed manual
Brakes:	Four-wheel discs
Body/chassis:	Fibreglass body with steel backbone chassis

UNITED KINGDOM

LOTUS ESPRIT TURBO

Once, 007 drove an Aston Martin. But during the 1970s and 1980s, he had a brand new super car to battle against the bad guys: the Lotus Esprit.

Styling was originally based on the 1972 Maserati Boomerang show car by Giorgetto Giugiaro. In 1987, the revised Esprit was restyled by designer Peter Stevens, and adopted a gentler, more rounded shape, although Lotus kept the new profile within 25 mm (one inch) of the old shape at all points.

Financial constraints at Lotus meant many components from other cars were used when the original Esprit was developed. The gearbox and final drive assembly came from a Citroën SM, while the Opel Ascona and Lancia Beta donated the front suspension and disc brakes respectively. And those streamlined door handles came from humble Morris Marina and Austin Allegro sedans.

The Esprit featured traditional Lotus trademarks. It had an exceptionally strong folded steel backbone chassis, onto which the fibreglass body was mounted, and pop-up headlamps, as pioneered by Lotus on the Elan.

Even though the engine was at the rear, the radiator was at the front – although steeply angled to fit under the sloping bonnet.

The engine was Lotus's own twin-cam four cylinder unit, mid-mounted at 45 degrees on the chassis for handling balance.

Name a supercar just as good under water as above it? If you believed the 1977 007 movie *The Spy Who Loved Me*, your answer would be the Lotus Esprit. What James Bond did for Aston Martin during the 1960s, Lotus hoped having 007 drive its apparently submersible Esprit would do for it a decade later. But the stunning-looking Esprit would have attracted attention anyway. The shape first appeared on a Maserati concept car from Italian stylist Giorgetto Giugiaro. It was a low, sleek and wide fibreglass creation, dramatic-looking, yet simple in its execution.

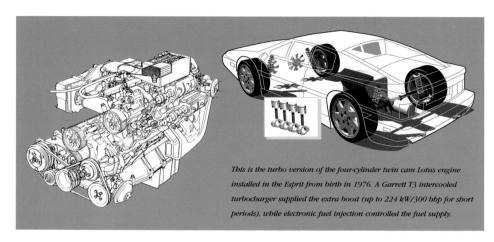

This is the turbo version of the four-cylinder twin cam Lotus engine installed in the Esprit from birth in 1976. A Garrett T3 intercooled turbocharger supplied the extra boost (up to 224 kW/300 bhp for short periods), while electronic fuel injection controlled the fuel supply.

Road revolution

Lotus engineers worked their own magic underneath. Their expertise conceived a car capable of handling and cornering like nothing else. Mounting a type 907 1,973 cc (120 ci) engine midway along the chassis, with all-independent suspension featuring racing car-like geometry, resulted in a vehicle that stuck to the road like glue.

When the production Esprit was launched in 1976, it was cheaper than its Italian rivals. But it was slower too, and suffered from reliability problems which harmed its reputation. Lotus worked hard to improve the Esprit. In 1978, the Series 2 arrived, with minor engine, wheel and cosmetic changes. It was followed by a volatile Turbo version two years later, and in 1981, the Series 3 burst on the scene, with a bigger 2,174 cc (132 ci) engine designed to finally unleash the Esprit's true potential.

When the shape started to look tired, Lotus embarked on a revamp. The 1987 Esprit was an impressive update, with a more curvaceous, modern-looking body. In 1996, a V8 engine replaced the four-cylinder unit, giving a huge increase in power.

Lotus Esprit Turbo

Top speed:	261 k/h (162 mph)
0-96 km/h (0-60 mph):	4.7 secs
Engine type:	In-line four
Displacement:	2,174 cc (132 ci)
Max power:	197 kW (264 bhp) @ 6,500 rpm
Max torque:	358 Nm (264 lb ft) @ 3,900 rpm
Weight:	1,204 kg (2,654 lb)
Economy:	7.43 km/l (21 mpg)
Transmission:	Five-speed manual
Brakes:	Vented discs all round, 26 cm (10.2 in) diameter at front, 27.4 cm (10.8 in) diameter at rear
Body/chassis:	Fibreglass body on galvanized steel backbone chassis

UNITED KINGDOM

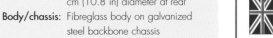

201

MASERATI GHIBLI

Although overshadowed by the Ferrari Daytona and Lamborghini Miura, the beautiful Maserati Ghibli is still one of the most stylish and charismatic supercars ever built.

Styling was by the great Giorgetto Giugiaro, when he was chief stylist at Ghia. He would go on to find more fame and fortune at Ital Design during the 1970s. The body is all steel. Despite its length, there's only room for two people inside the Ghibli's cabin.

The V8 engine was the most powerful Maserati had built. It was all-alloy, with four camshafts and four Weber carburettors to feed fuel at the rate of about one litre every 3.9 km (11 mpg). Still, if you could afford a Ghibli, you could afford the fuel.

Front and rear suspension was an interesting contrast. Wishbone front suspension was developed from Maserati racing principles, but at the rear, a traditional live rear axle on old-fashioned leaf springs was used.

Pop-up headlamps added to the Ghibli's wind-cheating lines.

125 Ghiblis were built as Spyder convertibles, compared to 1,149 coupés. The open cars are very desirable now because of their rarity, and change hands for enormous prices.

Vented disc brakes, with vacuum assistance, ensured the Ghibli was able to stop as well as it went.

ITALY

203

Like many cars, including Maserati stablemates the Bora and Mistral, the Ghibli is named after a wind. It's a good metaphor for the smooth-looking machine, capable of slicing across country at great speeds.

Maserati had once been a great racing team, with some legendary models bearing its trident badge over the years. That side of the company's exploits came to an end in 1957, largely because of financial problems and an unsuccessful Formula One effort.

Instead, Maserati turned to road cars, using its racing technology and immense V8 engines to build some very good machines. However, all of these would be eclipsed by the unveiling of the impressively-looking Ghibli in 1966.

The Ghibli V8 can be traced back to Maserati's racing engines of the 1950s. It was made of alloy, with wet iron cylinder liners attached to the block. There were four overhead camshafts.

The Ghibli was based on the previous Mexico model, but used a shortened chassis and a more powerful V8 engine. It kept this at the front of the car, despite moves by other manufacturers like Lamborghini towards mid-mounted units.

Early Giugiaro masterpiece

Conventional underneath it may have been, but all this was well-hidden underneath Giorgetto Giugiaro's stunning bodywork. It was – and still is – generally acknowledged to be the most beautiful Maserati ever, and its designer was rightly proud of it.

Sales were good, with more orders than could be fulfilled, and it even outsold chief rivals the Ferrari Daytona and the Lamborghini Miura, despite being mechanically less competent. The model was enhanced by the addition of the pretty convertible Spyder in 1969, which also received universal acclaim. Power was increased for the larger Ghibli SS in 1970.

However, by this time, the Ghibli's days were almost over. Maserati put its first mid-engined car, the Bora, into production in 1971, leaving the Ghibli to retire gracefully in 1973.

Maserati Ghibli

Top speed:	248 km/h (154 mph)
0-96 km/h (0-60mph):	6.8 secs
Engine type:	V8
Displacement:	4,719 cc (288 ci)
Max power:	276 kW (370 bhp) @ 5,500 rpm
Max torque:	441 Nm (326 lb ft) @ 4,000 rpm
Weight:	1,702 kg (3,745 lb)
Economy:	3.9 km/l (11 mpg)
Transmission:	Five-speed manual
Brakes:	Vented discs at front, solid discs at rear
Body:	Steel two-door 2+2 coupé with tubular-steel chassis

ITALY

205

MAZDA RX-7

Most manufacturers gave up on the rotary engine. Mazda stuck with the technology though, finally getting the success it deserved with the sporty RX-7.

The rotary engine design has fewer moving parts than a conventional engine and no pistons, so power delivery is smoother. It put out 75 kW (100 bhp) in standard form, but in 1983, a turbocharged version became available, with a power output of 123 kW (165 bhp). The chief handicaps of the design – once reliability problems had been ironed out – were poor fuel consumption and inferior pulling power from low speeds.

The RX7 design was done in-house at Mazda by a styling team overseen by Matasaburo Maeda. The look they were striving for was one of universal appeal and the simple, neat RX-7 shape achieved that aim.

The plunging hood line was only possible thanks to the compact rotary engine. It was installed well back in the bay, to give excellent weight distribution between the front and the rear, and enhance handling.

Retractable headlamps added to the RX-7's sporty style.

The glass hatchback was originally intended to be a one-piece wraparound item. However, manufacturing economies resulted in the use of three separate glass panes for the production model.

JAPAN

Theory often does not work as well as practice. Such was the case with the rotary engine (RE), invented by Felix Wankel. On paper, the RE had so much more to offer than a conventional reciprocating engine, but in practice, it was beset by technical problems, centring around leaks in the combustion chamber and rotor tip wear. NSU had found to its cost how difficult it was to build a marketable rotary-engined car, when its otherwise brilliant Ro80 failed badly.

That left the Japanese firm of Mazda to go it alone with the technology. With such cars as the Cosmo 110S, R100, RX-2, 3 and 4, Mazda gradually addressed the reliability

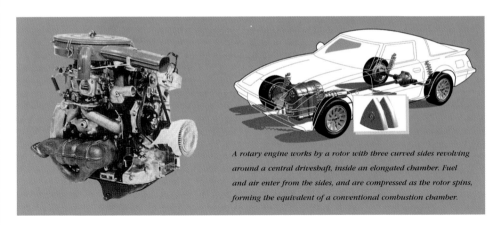

A rotary engine works by a rotor with three curved sides revolving around a central driveshaft, inside an elongated chamber. Fuel and air enter from the sides, and are compressed as the rotor spins, forming the equivalent of a conventional combustion chamber.

problems until, by the advent of the RX-7 in 1978, the twin-rotor engine finally reached its true potential.

Seven success

Mazda's lithe-looking sports car was a big sales winner, especially in America where the advanced, fresh styling, crisp performance, and most of all, the sparkling engine, won it many fans. Although the live-rear axle and MacPherson strut chassis was strictly orthodox, the RX-7 had responsive handling. Not since the Datsun 240Z had a car from the Far East seemed so much fun.

Its naturally handsome appearance meant that, over the seven years the first-generation RX-7 was in production, only a few minor cosmetic changes were needed to update the car. However, there were several mechanical enhancements, including a little more power in 1981, followed by a big power increase in 1983, with the electronically fuel-injected limited edition Turbo.

The new generation RX-7, still bearing a close resemblance to its illustrious forebear, replaced the original in 1985, after almost 500,000 had been built.

Mazda RX-7

Top speed:	193 km/h (120 mph)
0-96 km/h (0-60mph):	9.2 secs
Engine type:	Twin rotary
Displacement:	1,146 cc (70 ci)
Max power:	75 kW (100 bhp) @ 6,000 rpm
Max torque:	142 Nm (105 lb ft) @ 4,000 rpm
Weight:	1,091 kg (2,400 lb)
Economy:	9.8 km/l (27.6 mpg)
Transmission:	Five-speed manual
Brakes:	Discs, 27.9 cm (11 in) diameter at front, drums, 20.3 cm (8 in) diameter at rear
Body/chassis:	Steel monocoque with two-door hatchback coupé body

JAPAN

McLaren F1

F1 is a good name for McLaren's superlative road car. Just short of a full-blown Grand Prix racer, nothing else offered the same exhilaration or performance.

There was a hinged panel behind the rear hood. This was the 'brake-and-balance' foil, which automatically rose when the brakes were applied heavily. Its purpose was to stop the nose of the F1 diving.

Front luggage space was limited. However, McLaren cleverly added extra compartments between the doors and the rear wheels. The F1 was surprisingly practical.

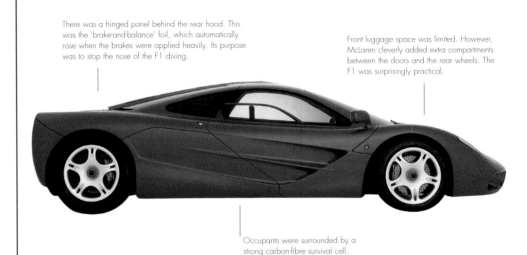

Occupants were surrounded by a strong carbon-fibre survival cell.

The seating arrangement was unusual. The driver's seat was in the centre, and set forward in the cockpit, with two passenger seats on either side and slightly behind. This position resulted in excellent visibility. A full racing harness was provided for the driver.

The central overhead spine gave the McLaren a distinctive look and also ducted air directly into the engine bay.

Big vents on the front of the F1 helped 'suck' the car towards the road. This is known as 'ground effect'.

The quad-cam V12 engine was lightweight, compact but extremely powerful. It was built for the F1 by BMW Motorsport. Power output was initially 410 kW (550 bhp), but rose to an awe-inspiring 498 kW (668 bhp).

UNITED KINGDOM

As the world's most expensive car, sales of the McLaren F1 were never going to be impressive. Any car which costs over \$1 million dollars is going to have a very limited appeal, but just 100 cars were built between 1992 and 1997, and less than 10 found their way to the US.

But financial success wasn't the point with the F1. Technical excellence, and sheer extravagance was. In the history of motoring, there has never been a car as wildly exotic as the F1, and there probably never will be again.

The man behind the F1 was racing designer Gordon Murray. Since the 1960s, he had wanted to build 'the pinnacle of 20th century high-performance car design'. But it was in the 1990s, after he had become

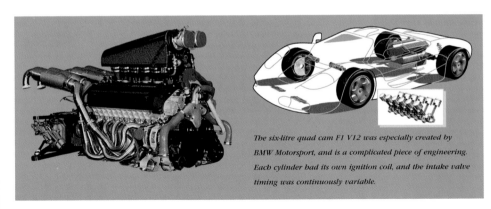

The six-litre quad cam F1 V12 was especially created by BMW Motorsport, and is a complicated piece of engineering. Each cylinder had its own ignition coil, and the intake valve timing was continuously variable.

technical director at the McLaren Formula One team that he got the chance.

Formula One on the road

Aside from managing the Grand Prix cars, Murray also set to work on using Formula One technology to create the ultimate road supercar. His goal was exceptional performance combined with practical usability. A new BMW engine was designed specifically for McLaren. The brief from McLaren was that it had to produce no fewer that 410 kW (550 bhp).

The F1 was unveiled at the Monaco Grand Prix in 1992, and production started the following year. In 1995, a tuned GTR version with 474 kW (636 bhp) was produced for racing, and won the 1996 Le Mans 24-hour race. In celebration, McLaren launched an even more powerful LM version, capable of 0-96 km/h (60 mph) in 3.2 seconds.

Following a revised GTR racer in 1997, the F1 went out of production only five years into its life, leaving an extraordinary legacy behind it.

McLaren F1

Top speed:	372 km/h (231 mph)
0-96 km/h (0-60 mph):	3.2 secs
Engine type:	V12
Displacement:	6,064 cc (370 ci)
Max power:	468 kW (627 bhp) @ 7,300 rpm
Max torque:	649 Nm (479 lb ft) @ 4,000 rpm
Weight:	1,020 kg (2,245 lb)
Economy:	4.4 km/l (12.4 mpg)
Transmission:	Six-speed manual
Brakes:	Four-wheel discs, 33.3 cm (13.1 in) diameter at front, 30.5 cm (12 in) diameter at rear
Body:	Carbon fibre two-door, three-seat coupé with carbon fibre and Nomex/alloy honeycomb monocoque chassis

UNITED KINGDOM

MERCEDES-BENZ 230-280SL

The 230-280SL range has timeless styling. Its uncluttered design still seems sharp even by today's standards, with the Pagoda roof giving it a distinctive look.

The cars came with a separate removable hardtop, which would become this SL's most famous feature. Its distinctive shape earned it the 'Pagoda' nickname. It took two people to lift off, although a roof hoist was an option.

Both manuals and automatics had four speeds. A four-speed manual gearbox was nothing unusual (in fact, it was rather dated – Mercedes-Benz would eventually offer an optional ZF five-speed transmission), but four speeds with an automatic was very advanced. Most other cars had just two or three.

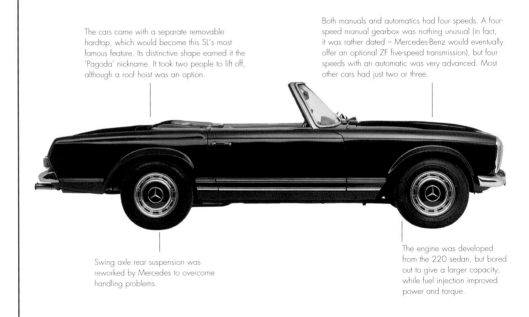

Swing axle rear suspension was reworked by Mercedes to overcome handling problems.

The engine was developed from the 220 sedan, but bored out to give a larger capacity, while fuel injection improved power and torque.

Stacked headlamps were a common Mercedes emblem, repeated on many of its cars throughout the 1960s.

Although technically a two-seater, there was the option of a third seat, which could be installed sideways in the rear!

Recirculating ball steering was less precise than rack-and-pinion, and was carried over from the 220 sedan, which donated its (shortened) floorpan to the new SL model.

GERMANY

The first generation of Mercedes-Benz SLs had been immensely desirable – but also extremely expensive. The next range of models to bear the name (known internally as W113) were more accessible to the common man, although deep pockets were still required for access to the exclusive SL club.

The 230SL was launched in 1963 at the Geneva Motor Show, always a good venue for capturing world attention. Compared to the previous 300SL, it had very understated looks, but it projected a sleek, ageless and extremely elegant appearance. This look was down to French designer Paul Bracq, who also came up with the unusually

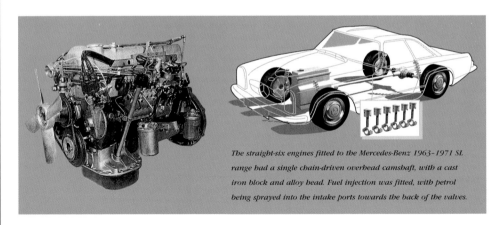

The straight-six engines fitted to the Mercedes-Benz 1963–1971 SL range had a single chain-driven overhead camshaft, with a cast iron block and alloy head. Fuel injection was fitted, with petrol being sprayed into the intake ports towards the back of the valves.

shaped Pagoda removable roof, so called because its large area of glass dictated a high, concave roof line and slim pillars.

Heavyweight lightweight

Although given the Super Light name, there was little lightweight about the car, based as it was on a shortened 220SE sedan. It was solidly engineered, but bulky, more a grand tourer than a true sports car. And it was well-equipped too, becoming the first Mercedes to feature disc brakes, initially just on the front wheels.

Major improvements came four years after launch, with the creation of the 250SL, featuring a tougher, bigger engine. A five-speed gearbox also became available for smoother high speed cruising. The 250SL did not last long, however; around 5,000 models were built before it was replaced a year later by the improved 280SL, with another increase in capacity.

The W113 series came to an end in 1971,

although it still looked fresh and up-to-date despite having been in production for almost a decade. The replacement SL drew on much of its relation's timeless styling, but added a V8 engine.

Mercedes-Benz SL (1962 230SL)

Top speed:	193 km/h (120 mph)
0-96 km/h (0-60 mph):	10.9 secs
Engine type:	In-line six
Displacement:	2,306 cc (141 ci)
Max power:	112 kW (150 bhp) @ 5,500 rpm
Max torque:	217 Nm (160 lb ft) @ 4,500 rpm
Weight:	1,330 kg (2,927 lb)
Economy:	5 km/l (14 mpg)
Transmission:	Five-speed manual or four-speed automatic
Brakes:	Four-wheel discs
Body/chassis:	Steel monocoque, two-door sports car body

GERMANY

MERCEDES-BENZ 300SL

The greatest classic car of all time? The 300SL consistently tops polls as the most sensational car ever. And it lives up to its reputation.

Cooling vents on the side of the car were reminiscent of gills, suitable for the slippery 300SL shape. The vents had to be made large to allow heat to escape from the engine bay.

High sills (required to cover the side of the space-frame chassis) helped dictate the use of gullwing doors, the most famous feature of the 300SL. They were made of alloy panels, to save stress on the roof-mounted hinges and to make them easier for occupants to open, of course.

Tilting steering wheels aren't common even today, but the 300SL had one to make entry and exit easier. This feature was known as 'the fat man's wheel'!

The engine was an improved version of that used in the 300 sedan, but slanted so the hood line was low. However, a bulge was provided to clear the fuel injection system. One was provided on the other side just for cosmetic balance. The injection system, by Bosch, was the first to be fitted to a production car, and boosted power to twice the original output of the engine.

GERMANY

219

GERMANY

Mercedes-Benz had been a major force in racing before World War II. It made an amazing return to motorsport in 1952 with the 300SL (standing for 'super light'). The gullwinged sensation won Le Mans at its first attempt, and went on to notch up many other impressive victories.

Perhaps even more electrifying than the racer itself was the news that Mercedes intended to put the 300SL into production as a mainstream road-going model. The road version was unveiled to an awestruck and enthusiastic public in February 1954, with full-scale manufacture getting under way the following year.

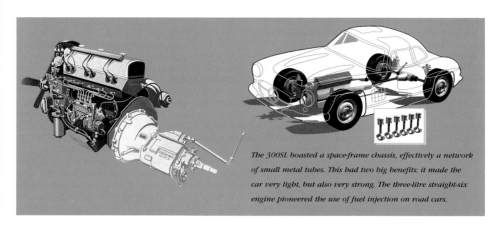

The 300SL boasted a space-frame chassis, effectively a network of small metal tubes. This had two big benefits: it made the car very light, but also very strong. The three-litre straight-six engine pioneered the use of fuel injection on road cars.

Race track to roadway

The road-going 300SL was a stunning sight. The exquisite body was crafted in steel with alloy panels. Underneath was a complicated space-frame chassis, made of slim tubing. Such a system hadn't been featured on a road car before and neither has it been used since. The gullwing doors were retained, due to the deep sills on the car. There were a few fussy cosmetic details, like the 'eyebrows' above the wheel arches, but overall, it was a wonderfully pure shape.

The engine itself was quite ordinary – a development from the 300 sedan – but the mechanical fuel-injection system it used was radical, another production first. It turned the SL into a superb performer, faster even than the racing cars from which it originated.

The gullwing SL had a short production life. Just 1,400 were made before a more conventional open roadster, with a redesigned chassis, appeared at the Geneva Motor Show in 1957. It was more powerful and practical, but somehow had less appeal than its predecessor.

Manufacture ended in 1963, after a removable hardtop was made available in 1958, and all-round disc brakes in 1961.

Mercedes-Benz 300SL

Top speed:	266 km/h (165 mph)
0-96 km/h (0-60 mph):	9.0 secs
Engine type:	In-line six
Displacement:	2,996 cc (183 ci)
Max power:	179 kW (240 bhp) @ 6,100 rpm
Max torque:	293 Nm (216 lb ft) @ 4,800 rpm
Weight:	1,295 kg (2,850 lb)
Economy:	6.4 km/l (18 mpg)
Transmission:	Four-speed manual
Brakes:	Four-wheel drums
Body/chassis:	Steel and alloy two-door coupé with steel space-frame chassis

GERMANY

MERCURY COUGAR

Stretching the Mustang into a Mercury was a brave step. It could have backfired badly, but instead, the Cougar joined the muscle car hall of fame.

The V8 engines for the 1967 to 1973 Mercury Cougars varied from 4,736 cc (289 ci) up to the terrifying 7,014 cc (428 ci) Cobra Jet, capable of producing 250 kW (335 bhp). This car has the latter unit installed.

The Cougar was similar to its smaller Mustang cousin in many ways, including the huge list of optional extras. 'High impact' exterior colours included bright blue, orange and yellow, while the GT-E package featured a massive 7,014 cc (428 ci) V8 with bonnet scoops. And if you wanted to be really seen, there was even a Paisley vinyl roof option!

Cougars came with three-speed transmissions as standard, with a four-speed manual gearbox or three-speed automatic also available.

The headlamps were concealed behind a slatted grille, which would flip up automatically when the headlamps were turned on. They were vacuum operated.

The indicators on the back end were sequential, as also found on the Ford Thunderbird and Shelby Mustang. They are combined with the brake lights, and would flash in sequence when the direction switch was operated.

UNITED STATES

223

UNITED STATES

The Mercury brand was seen as a middle of the road alternative to the cheap and cheerful Ford brand and the exclusive Lincoln range. It was never a major seller. That is, not until the release of the upmarket Mustang muscle car contender in 1967.

The 'pony car' market invented by the Mustang in 1964 was such a buoyant one that Ford felt it could add an upmarket car to the mix. Mercury was chosen to be the badge it wore, with the animal-named Cougar of 1967 essentially a stretched version of the successful Ford, with more

Underneath the bood of the Cougar Eliminator was either a 302 V8 or a 428 Cobra Jet (left), also used in the Mustang. This was the high-performance engine in the range, and came with or without ram-air induction. Customers could also specify different carburettor set-ups.

home comforts inside. Like the Mustang, it came with a comprehensive range of optional extras, and also shared the same forceful V8s. But it also had a distinctive, brawny look all of its own, thanks to its bulging flanks and slatted front and rear bodywork with concealed lights.

It wasn't quite the extraordinary success of the Mustang, but sales of 150,000 in 1967 and 110,000 the following year were healthy enough, and the Cougar was *Motor Trend*'s Car of the Year too.

From pony to puny

A continual policy of improvement resulted in a more powerful engine being installed for 1968, including the XR-7G, named after racer Dan Gurney. The Cougar got wider, longer and heavier for 1969, but the all-conquering and none-too-subtle Eliminator package put it at the forefront of the muscle car power pack. A convertible hit the streets as well.

The Eliminator was dropped the following year after 2,200 had been sold. The 1971 Cougars got bigger still, with the emphasis starting to shift towards luxury instead of sporting prowess, with the last true pony car Cougar appearing in 1973.

Mercury Cougar

Top speed:	171 km/h (106 mph)
0-96 km/h (0-60 mph):	5.6 secs
Engine type:	V8
Displacement:	7,014 cc (428 ci)
Max power:	250 kW (335 bhp) @ 5,200 rpm
Max torque:	596 Nm (440 lb ft) @ 3,400 rpm
Weight:	1,718 kg (3,780 lb)
Economy:	2.2 km/l (6.2 mpg)
Transmission:	C6 Cruise-O-Matic
Brakes:	Discs at front, drums at rear
Body:	Steel monocoque two-door coupé body

UNITED STATES

MGB

The MGB, either as Roadster or GT, is one of the most enduring classics ever, and redefined the British sports car experience during the 1960s.

The BMC B-series engine was developed from the previous MGA model, but enlarged to 1,798 cc (110 ci). Although the power output would vary over the 18 years the MGB was in production, the displacement would stay the same. However, a six-cylinder MGB appeared from 1967 to 1969, and a GT V8 from 1973 to 1976, but neither was as successful as the four-cylinder cars.

The first MGBs were all roadsters. It wasn't until 1965 that the enclosed GT version arrived.

Steel wheels and alloys were available at varying times during the MGB's career, but the cars always looked best with traditional wire wheels, especially if they were glistening chrome.

Windscreens had a bar down the centre, used for mounting the rear-view mirror. —

The MGB was the first monocoque construction MG sports car.

Chrome bumpers were fitted up until 1974, when US Federal regulations dictated a change to bulky polyurethane items (known as 'rubber bumper models') capable of withstanding an 8 km/h (5 mph) collision. The ride height also had to be raised too, by 4.4 cm (1.75 in), a move which adversely affected the handling.

Few sports cars have met with such universal approval as that enduring British classic, the MGB. It has become the epitome of the typical British sports car, the benchmark by which all others are judged.

Once upon a time, MGs were strictly for the traditional, no frills type of customer. The B, though, was totally up-to-date, and excellent value for money. It had great looks, didn't cost a fortune to buy or run and could boast a reasonable level of performance.

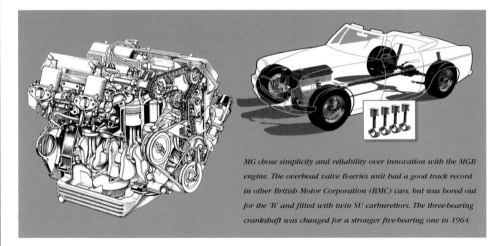

MG chose simplicity and reliability over innovation with the MGB engine. The overhead valve B-series unit had a good track record in other British Motor Corporation (BMC) cars, but was bored out for the 'B' and fitted with twin SU carburettors. The three-bearing crankshaft was changed for a stronger five-bearing one in 1964.

And marketing it with the slogan 'Your mother wouldn't like it' instantly endeared it to the young and the young at heart.

Sporting history

Introduced in 1962, the original open two-seater roadster was joined by the GT, a pretty fixed-head coupé (styled with some help from Pininfarina), in 1965. When the Austin-Healey 3000 – another one of America's favourite British sports cars – was dropped, a three-litre (183 ci) engine was used to create the MGC as a successor. Despite the considerable extra power, sales were disappointing, as they were for the later MGB GT V8, which could not be sold in the US due to emissions problems.

After big black 'rubber' bumpers were fitted throughout the range in 1974, the writing was on the wall for the MGB. The end for one of the world's best-loved sports cars came a few years later in 1980, but the movement that had grown up around these cars is still huge today. You do not just drive this tremendously entertaining yet wonderfully affordable icon, you live the life that comes with it, too.

MGB

Top speed:	169 km/h (105 mph)
0-96 km/h (0-60 mph):	12.5 secs
Engine type:	In-line four
Displacement:	1,798 cc (110 ci)
Max power:	71 kW (95 bhp) @ 5,500 rpm
Max torque:	149 Nm (110 lb ft) @ 3,500 rpm
Weight:	946 kg (2,080 lb)
Economy:	6.9 km/l (19.6 mpg)
Transmission:	Four-speed manual (overdrive optional)
Brakes:	Discs at front, drums at rear
Body/chassis:	Monocoque chassis with two-door steel open body

MITSUBISHI LANCER EVO

The various Lancer Evos have become celebrated as among the best ever rally cars. They may look like standard models, but mechanically, they're radically different.

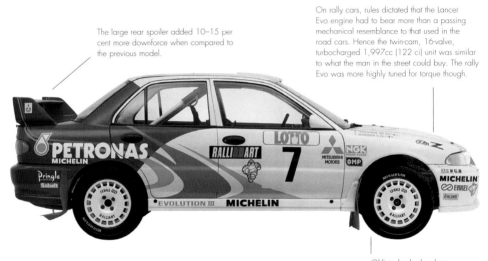

The large rear spoiler added 10–15 per cent more downforce when compared to the previous model.

On rally cars, rules dictated that the Lancer Evo engine had to bear more than a passing mechanical resemblance to that used in the road cars. Hence the twin-cam, 16-valve, turbocharged 1,997cc (122 ci) unit was similar to what the man in the street could buy. The rally Evo was more highly tuned for torque though.

Ohlins shock absorbers were adjustable for great handling. They did cost £2,500 each, though.

A six-speed transmission was fitted, together with computer-controlled differentials which varied the amount of torque sent to each wheel, depending on the road surface.

A large roll cage was fitted inside the competition Evo. It wasn't just for occupant protection, but also stiffened the bodyshell and provided more solid suspension mounting points.

The massive front air dam was a risky fitting. While it helped with cooling and aerodynamics, it was easily damaged during rough rally conditions. Few Evos managed to finish a rally with the air dam completely intact.

JAPAN

In 1998, Mitsubishi finally got the result it had been striving for since it first entered the World Rally Championship 24 years earlier. The WRC Manufacturer's title was taken at last, along with the Drivers' championship laurels, and the Re-N World Driver prize. It was a complete sweep of all the WRC crowns. And the car responsible for this complete dominance of the 1998 rally season? The Mitsubishi Lancer Evo.

The first Lancer was introduced in February 1973. It entered rallying the same year, notching up some notable successes. This competition career continued through the various incarnations of the Lancer (the

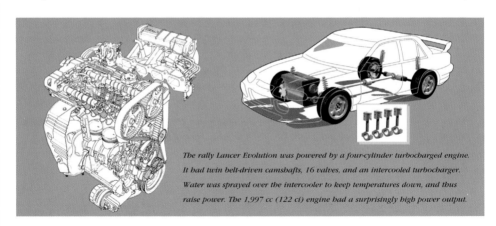

The rally Lancer Evolution was powered by a four-cylinder turbocharged engine. It had twin belt-driven camshafts, 16 valves, and an intercooled turbocharger. Water was sprayed over the intercooler to keep temperatures down, and thus raise power. The 1,997 cc (122 ci) engine had a surprisingly high power output.

Mk II in 1979, a Turbo in 1981, a Mk III for 1984 and the Mk IV in 1988), but it wasn't until 1992 that things got really serious, with the Evolution I model.

Evolution of the species

The road Evolutions were built as rally homologation cars, primarily for the Japanese market. Only a few went abroad, either officially or as personal imports. That scarcity, plus the unparalleled excellence of the Evo on the international rallying scene, soon earned the car legendary status. Either in competition, or on the road, a Lancer Evo offered stunning turbocharged acceleration, plus masterful handling thanks to its all-wheel drive. And it looked the business too, thanks to its aerodynamic aids, body kit and gaping air vents.

Living up to its name, the Evo evolved through several versions, each one seeming to become more successful than the last. The Evo III was the first to win the WRC

Drivers' championship in 1996 for Tommi Makinen, who also won in 1997 and 1998. Today's Evo VII is still as superb as ever.

Mitsubishi Lancer Evo (Evo III)

Top speed:	200 km/h (124 mph)
0-96 km/h (0-60 mph):	3.5 secs
Engine type:	In-line four
Displacement:	1,997 cc (122 ci)
Max power:	220 kW (295 bhp) @ 6,500 rpm
Max torque:	501 Nm (370 lb ft) @ 5,000 rpm
Weight:	1,233 kg (2,712 lb)
Economy:	n/a
Transmission:	Six-speed manual with four-wheel drive and triple disc carbon clutch
Brakes:	Four-wheel vented discs, 31.0 cm (12.2 in) diameter at front, 27.9 cm (11 in) diameter at rear
Body/chassis:	Unitary construction steel four-wheel saloon

JAPAN

MORRIS MINOR

Ford's Model T, the Volkswagen Beetle, the Citroën 2CV ... and the Morris Minor. The charming 'poached egg on wheels' was Britain's first true people's car.

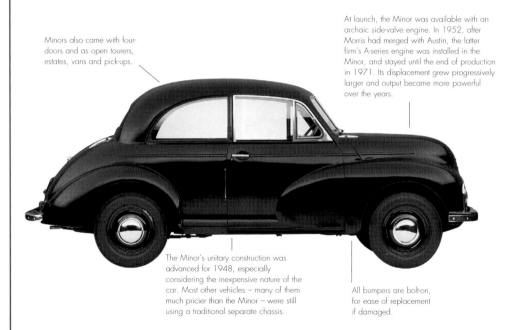

Minors also came with four-doors and as open tourers, estates, vans and pick-ups.

At launch, the Minor was available with an archaic side-valve engine. In 1952, after Morris had merged with Austin, the latter firm's A-series engine was installed in the Minor, and stayed until the end of production in 1971. Its displacement grew progressively larger and output became more powerful over the years.

The Minor's unitary construction was advanced for 1948, especially considering the inexpensive nature of the car. Most other vehicles – many of them much pricier than the Minor – were still using a traditional separate chassis.

All bumpers are bolt-on, for ease of replacement if damaged.

The low-line headlamp look only lasted until 1950, when lighting regulations forced a change. Thereafter, the lamp units were mounted on the front bumpers.

The ridge down the front and gap in the front bumper was due to designer Alec Issigonis cutting a prototype in half and widening the car by 10 cm (4 in), just before production started.

Trafficator indicators were never fitted to American cars, which always had flashing direction lights.

UNITED KINGDOM

235

MORRIS MINOR

The Minor name was first used during the 1920s but it was eclipsed by the car which revived the tag in 1948. The 'new' Minor, designed by Alec Issigonis, the stylist also responsible for the Mini, may have looked like a 'poached egg' according to the boss of the Morris company, Lord Nuffield, but the public, it seemed, loved eggs. Over its 23-year production life, more than 1.5 million cars were sold, and it became the first British car to sell over a million units.

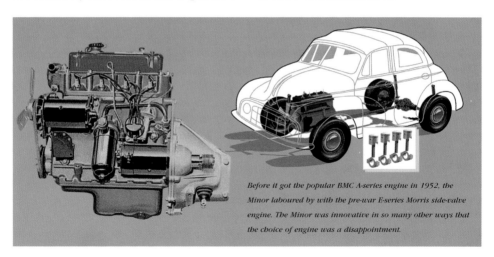

Before it got the popular BMC A-series engine in 1952, the Minor laboured by with the pre-war E-series Morris side-valve engine. The Minor was innovative in so many other ways that the choice of engine was a disappointment.

What made it so popular? Well, like its Beetle and 2CV contemporaries, it was reliable, cheap, pleasant to drive and well thought out. Most of all though, it seemed to have a big personality that endeared it to all. It was truly classless, the very definition of a people's car.

Development began during the war, during which time the car was referred to as the Mosquito. It was launched at the first post-war London Motor Show to much praise, one motoring magazine even saying it 'approached perfection'.

Bigger and better

If there was one major fault, it was the lacklustre pre-war side-valve engine. However, this was replaced by Austin's better A-series unit in 1952 (much to the chagrin of Morris employees, who didn't want a rival's engine powering their baby). The A-series was enlarged in 1956 (to make the Morris 1000) and again in 1962.

By the time production ended in 1971, the Minor had become a British icon. A large and loyal enthusiast base ensures it is still a common sight today throughout the British Isles.

Morris Minor (1949 series)

Top speed:	100 km/h (62 mph)
0-96 km/h (0-60 mph):	52 secs
Engine type:	Side-valve four
Displacement:	918 cc (56 ci)
Max power:	21 kW (28 bhp) @ 4,400 rpm
Max torque:	53 Nm (39 lb ft) @ 2,400 rpm
Weight:	793 kg (1,745 lb)
Economy:	12.7 km/l (36 mpg)
Transmission:	Four-speed manual
Brakes:	Four-wheel drums
Body/chassis:	Unitary monocoque construction with steel sedan, convertible and estate bodies

NSU Ro80

The rotary-engined NSU Ro80 was a bold automotive design on all levels. However, persistent problems with its innovative engine would ultimately result in its downfall.

Designer Claus Luthe and project co-ordinator Ewald Praxl were responsible for the aerodynamic wedge shape. Luthe penned the styling without using a wind tunnel; only when the car was finished was it subjected to aerodynamic tests. Pictures of those experiments would later appear in advertising material for the car.

The 'Ro' in Ro80 stands for rotary. The engineering principle was the brainchild of Felix Wankel, and dates from the 1940s. Instead of pistons and valves, triangular rotors move in a housing with curved ends and straight sides. This set-up delivers exceptionally smooth power, but rotor tip life was short on the Ro80, and fuel consumption poor.

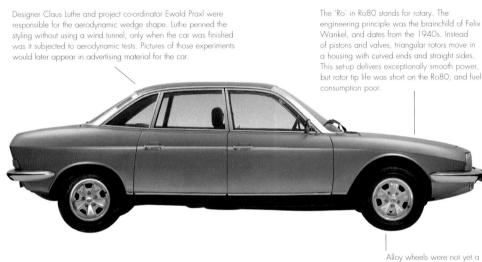

Alloy wheels were not yet a common sight on sedans.

Power steering was essential on the Ro80. The engine was mounted ahead of the front axle, making the car very nose-heavy.

The Ro80 had a three-speed semi-automatic transmission, which made the already bad fuel consumption even worse.

Disc brakes all around ensured the Ro80 was capable of stopping easily. MacPherson strut suspension on all wheels also meant a comfortable ride with good handling.

In 1968, the NSU Ro80 was awarded the European Car of the Year accolade. Yet, within a few years, sales would plummet, and the car would be out of production within a decade. Where did it all go so wrong for the revolutionary vehicle which could have changed the future of motoring?

The rotary engine design, which dispensed with valves, pistons and camshafts, came from Felix Wankel. After years of development, he sold his ideas to the German NSU company who created the world's first rotary engined production car, the diminutive Spider of 1964.

There are few moving parts in a rotary engine, which should make it more reliable. However, that was not the case with the Ro80 unit. Problems included rotor tip wear, and sealing the rotor and tips to the housing.

A far more ambitious vehicle followed in 1967. The Ro80 was years ahead of its time, a big sedan with distinctive styling and clever engineering, including disc brakes, a semi-automatic clutchless gearbox, front-wheel drive and an innovative independent strut suspension.

Flawed genius

But the real finesse lay under the hood. The rotary engine design meant an incredibly smooth power delivery, and although rated at just 995 cc (61 ci), the twin rotors inside meant it was the equivalent of a conventional 1990 cc (121 ci) car. Total output was a good 86 kW (115 bhp).

As innovative as it was, the technology hadn't been perfected. Rotor tip wear meant that engines would often fail after just 32,000 km (20,000 miles). NSU persisted, but falling sales coupled with crippling warranty claims brought the company to its knees. It was taken over by Volkswagen in

1969, who finally dropped the brilliant but troublesome car in 1977.

NSU Ro80

Top speed:	177 k/h (110 mph)
0-96 km/h (0-60 mph):	13.4 secs
Engine type:	Wankel rotary
Displacement:	995 cc (61 ci)
Max power:	86 kW (115 bhp) @ 5,500 rpm
Max torque:	164 Nm (121 lb ft) @ 4,500 rpm
Weight:	1,225 kg (2,695 lb)
Economy:	5.6 km/l (15.7 mpg)
Transmission:	Three-speed semi-automatic with torque convertor
Brakes:	Four-wheel discs, 28.2 cm (11.1 in) diameter at front, 27.2 cm (10.7 in) diameter at rear
Body/chassis:	Steel monocoque with four-door sedan body

GERMANY

PLYMOUTH HEMI 'CUDA

The Barracuda finally became a muscle car legend in 1970, when it appeared with the mighty Hemi V8 and a selection of equally outrageous colours.

A bright range of loud and proud 'High Impact' colours was available for the 'Cuda, including Lime Light Green, Violet, Lemon Twist and Vitamin C.

A standard feature was the 'Shaker' hood, with the air cleaner poking up through a cut-out. Usually painted in a different colour from the rest of the car, it vibrated with the engine running, and was a real attention grabber ... except in California, where it was banned because of drive-by noise rules!

If the 1970 'Cuda looks a little familiar, that's because the styling was shared with the Dodge Challenger. However, the 'Cuda was much more of an audacious performer, in both looks and performance. Convertibles were also available, but only 14 were made in 1970.

This 'Cuda has been sympathetically customized. The most obvious alterations are the huge rear tyres, about twice the width of the originals.

'Hemi' refers to the hemispherical combustion chambers in the 426 V8, intended to produce more efficient combustion of the gas/air mixture.

Rectangular exhaust tail pipes fitted in the rear valance were a neat touch of style.

Chrysler tried to steal Ford's thunder with the Barracuda. It hit the streets two weeks ahead of the Mustang in 1964, pitched at the same youth market. But it would never scale the sales heights achieved by the Blue Oval pony car.

A big factor in its comparative failure was the gawky fastback styling, which made it look old-fashioned too quickly, unlike the Mustang. 1967's restyle improved matters, both in stylistic and mechanical terms. The pony Plymouth looked meaner, projected more attitude, and finally looked like it could take on a Mustang or Camaro. The new 6,276 cc (383 ci) V8 meant it had the performance to take them on too.

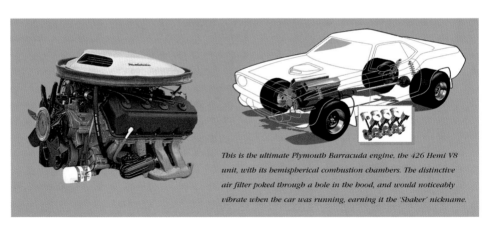

This is the ultimate Plymouth Barracuda engine, the 426 Hemi V8 unit, with its hemispherical combustion chambers. The distinctive air filter poked through a hole in the hood, and would noticeably vibrate when the car was running, earning it the 'Shaker' nickname.

But it would be in 1970 that the Barracuda finally became a true great. Using Chrysler's E-body – shared with the Dodge Challenger – the new Plymouth for the new decade was an all-out street racer. Performance models were known as 'Cudas, the slang abbreviation being coined by street rodders. They were easily recognizable by being the most garishly painted vehicles on the road, the theory being that if you've got it, you might as well flaunt it.

Hemi hero

Nine engines were available, but there was only one for those interested in out-dragging anything else on the highway: the race-bred 6,981 cc (426 ci) Hemi V8, with an huge 317 kW (425 bhp) on tap. It had enough acceleration to make an Apollo moon rocket look lethargic.

It was an all too brief high point for Plymouth though. The Hemi disappeared in 1972, unable to meet new emissions standards. The Barracuda became more emasculated as the decade progressed and by 1975 it was no longer a performance car, and the Hemi 'Cuda was just a fond memory.

Plymouth Hemi 'Cuda

Top speed:	220 km/h (137 mph)
0-96 km/h (0-60mph):	4.3 secs
Engine type:	V8
Displacement:	7,079 cc (432 ci)
Max power:	462 kW (620 bhp) @ 6,500 rpm
Max torque:	887.5 Nm (655 lb ft) @ 5,100 rpm
Weight:	1,793 kg (3,945 lb)
Economy:	3.3 km/l (9.4 mpg)
Transmission:	Chrysler A-833 four-speed manual
Brakes:	Discs at front, drums at rear
Body/chassis:	Steel monocoque two-door coupé body

UNITED STATES

245

PLYMOUTH SUPERBIRD

Subtle, understated, shy and retiring ... all words which could not be applied to the utterly over-the-top Plymouth Superbird, a colourful exercise in racing brashness.

Superbirds were based on the Plymouth Road Runner, and showed their origins by the cartoon Road Runner decals on the side and front. Even the horn went 'meep meep' just like the Warner Bros character!

The 'droop snoot' front was not only aerodynamic, but also added downforce. It was made of fibreglass, and had pop-up headlamps to preserve its wind-cheating benefits. It added 43 cm (17 in) to the car's length.

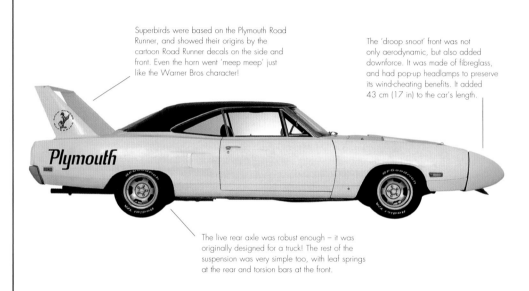

The live rear axle was robust enough – it was originally designed for a truck! The rest of the suspension was very simple too, with leaf springs at the rear and torsion bars at the front.

The rear wing was a dramatic feature, but was mounted high so that air-flow over it was less disturbed, and so the trunk could be opened. The angle was adjustable to vary the level of downforce, but needed precise positioning to be effective.

The Chrysler V8 'Hemi' engine was standard on racing Superbirds, optional on the road cars. The Hemi name was derived from the hemispherical combustion chambers, which gave a large valve area, but was more complicated to build.

UNITED STATES

247

Wylie E Coyote never caught the Road Runner. Whatever ACME tricks he tried, none of them worked. He shouldn't have bothered with gimmicks. He should have just bought an example of the car that bore the name of his arch-nemesis, and used that to catch him. Road Runner the bird would not have stood a chance.

The Plymouth Road Runner Superbird was one of America's most spectacular vehicles ever. From its pointed front to its huge rear spoiler, the often garishly coloured Superbird was an attention-grabber. It was created to dominate NASCAR racing, not only to boost car sales but also to beat Ford.

Ford was the master of the track, and although Chrysler had the engines to beat

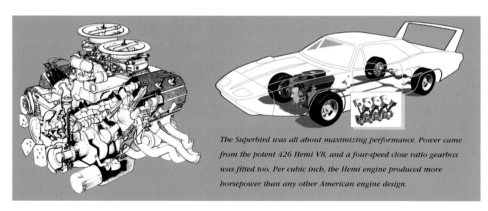

The Superbird was all about maximizing performance. Power came from the potent 426 Hemi V8, and a four-speed close ratio gearbox was fitted too. Per cubic inch, the Hemi engine produced more horsepower than any other American engine design.

the blue oval, it did not have a sufficiently aerodynamic car. Its first solution was to clean up the Dodge Charger in 1969, with smoother bodywork and a big rear wing, calling the result the Charger Daytona. 1,200 cars would also go to the public.

Hatching the Superbird

Success encouraged Chrysler to build the visually similar Plymouth Superbird for 1970, based on the stock Road Runner. This model would sell 1,971 units, with 6,981 cc (426 ci) Hemi or 7,210 cc (440 ci) engine options, with either a four-barrel or three two-barrel carburettors.

More significantly, racing Superbirds capable of over 322 km/h (200 mph) would go on to take 21 Grand National wins, including the Daytona 500. Ford's stranglehold on the track had been broken.

The Superbird's career was short. NASCAR regulations changed for 1971, demanding a reduction in the size of its engines. Chrysler preferred to let the Superbird go out in a blaze of glory.

Plymouth Superbird

Top speed:	225 km/h (140 mph)
0-96 km/h (0-60mph):	6.1 secs
Engine type:	V8
Displacement:	6,981 cc (426 ci)
Max power:	317 kW (425 bhp) @ 5,000 rpm
Max torque:	664 Nm (490 lb ft) @ 4,000 rpm
Weight:	1,582 kg (3,487 lb)
Economy:	4.9 km/l (13.8 mpg)
Transmission:	Torqueflite three-speed auto plus torque convertor or Mopar 883 four-speed manual
Brakes:	Vented discs, 27.9 cm (11 in) diameter at front, drums, 27.9 cm (11 in) diameter at rear
Body/chassis:	Steel channel chassis welded to body with bolted front subframe

UNITED STATES

PONTIAC GTO

Regarded as the first real muscle car, the letters G, T and O are the three most evocative letters in the alphabet for American enthusiasts.

The Judge-spec GTO came with a 273 kW (366 bhp) Ram Air III V8. However, customers could also get the extreme Ram Air IV engine. It was quoted as only offering 3 kW (4 bhp) more, but this figure was understated.

This is not just an ordinary third generation GTO. It is one of the outrageous Judge models, characterized by bright paintwork, blue and yellow striping, a trunk spoiler and Judge logos.

GTOs had a heavy-duty suspension, firmed up by stiffer springs and shock absorbers, as well as an anti-roll bar. However, drum brakes remained standard, although front discs were an option.

The hood-mounted tachometer was a GTO talking point. Through the windscreen, it was dead ahead of the driver, ensuring he could keep an eye on it at all times. Its usefulness was diminished in rain or cold weather though, when it could become difficult to see.

As new safety regulations began to bite, the GTO was one of the first homegrown cars to be fitted with energy-absorbing bumpers. The Endura nose could withstand a knock of up to 6.5 km/h (4 mph).

UNITED STATES

251

UNITED STATES

Had it not been for the Ford Mustang stealing its thunder, the Pontiac GTO might have become universally known as the first muscle car. The production of the GTO pre-dated the fast Ford by a few months, yet would be overshadowed by its Blue Oval rival.

In 1963, General Motors put a sudden stop on its divisions putting big engines into intermediate models. Over at Pontiac, they had other plans. Chief engineer John DeLorean, with the support of boss Bunkie Knudsen, shoehorned a massive V8 into its standard Tempest, to make the Tempest GTO.

The GTO Judge was only available for three years. It came with suitably extreme engines, with the standard item being a 6,554 cc (400 ci) Ram Air III V8, with D-port cylinder heads, a hydraulic camshaft, free-flow exhaust manifolds and a Rochester Quadrajet carburettor. Even more outrageous was the Ram IV 400 V8.

The car was a scintillating performer, although some eyebrows were raised at the use of the GTO name, *Road & Track* magazine referring to the steal from Ferrari as 'an act of unforgivable dishonesty'.

America's Ferrari?

Nevertheless, those who couldn't afford an Italian GTO found that the American pretender came much cheaper and was almost as much fun, even if it didn't quite have the same exotic looks.

The Pontiac became its own model in 1966, for which it got a restyle with flowing 'coke bottle' lines. Two years later, there was another revamp, setting the GTO up for its onslaught on the 1970s. Impact-resistant Endura bumpers were fitted, their strength being demonstrated in a commercial where John DeLorean attacked them with a sledgehammer. And hidden headlamps were an option specified by many. Less common was the Judge performance pack, which combined a garish livery with Pontiac's most powerful V8 engine to create a true muscle car spectacular.

Amid growing automotive regulations, the GTO disappeared in 1974, little more than a name on other Pontiac models by that time.

Pontiac GTO

Top speed:	198 km/h (123 mph)
0-96 km/h (0-60mph):	6.2 secs
Engine type:	V8
Displacement:	6,554 cc (400 ci)
Max power:	273 kW (366 bhp) @ 5,400 rpm
Max torque:	603 Nm (445 lb ft) @ 3,600 rpm
Weight:	1,592 kg (3,503 lb)
Economy:	3.9 km/l (11 mpg)
Transmission:	Muncie M-21 four-speed manual
Brakes:	Discs at front, drums at rear
Body/chassis:	Separate steel chassis with two-door coupé body

UNITED STATES

PONTIAC TRANS AM

Unlike many of its muscle car competitors, Pontiac's Trans Am managed to weather the troublesome years of the 1970s without its performance becoming too compromised.

The front air dam and sloping plastic impact-resistant front added to the Trans Am's stability and aerodynamics, but also gave it a moody, brooding character.

Flared wheel arches were an essential 1970s look, if you wanted to make it obvious that a car had real attitude.

To reflect over-protective times, the Trans Am's former 257 km/h (160 mph) speedo just went to 161 km/h (100 mph) by 1975.

Powering the Pontiac Trans Am until 1976 was the High Output 7,456 cc (455 ci) V8, reputedly the largest engine ever fitted on a muscle car. Although the engine had been discontinued by the time this 1978 model appeared, this car has been retro-fitted with one of these mighty power plants, as evidenced by the 455 badging on the bonnet scoop.

Trans Ams hoods wore a distinctive 'screaming chicken' decal. It was meant to represent an updated version of the Native American phoenix symbol, and was penned by stylist John Schinella.

Despite its considerable performance potential – around 217 km/h (135 mph) in ideal conditions – the Trans Am retained drum brakes at the rear, although disc brakes were fitted at the front.

UNITED STATES

UNITED STATES

Despite the popularity of its GTO, Pontiac was still envious of the success of Ford's Mustang and Chevrolet's Camaro. So in 1967, Pontiac launched its own true pony car, the Firebird. Available with both six-cylinder and V8 engines, there was much Mustang and Camaro influence in the resulting creation, although the styling was more European than American.

The look of the Firebird was reworked for 1969, and for mid-year, the Trans Am Performance and Appearance Package was quietly launched. Firebird Trans Ams were instantly recognizable by their Polar White bodywork, blue racing stripes, adjustable

Various V8 engines were fitted to the Trans Am during its life. But this example sports the most excessive engine of all. The 455 V8 was allegedly the biggest engine ever fitted on an American muscle car. This one has been modified for extra performance.

hood air intakes, rear spoiler and big Ram Air III or IV V8 engines.

1970s style

The Trans Am became a model in its own right in 1970, and once again there was a restyle. The 1970s look was brawny and loud, the Trans Am oozing attitude from every muscular metal curve. Endura rubber bumpers dispensed with the need for conventional items at the front, giving the Trans Am even more of a purposeful guise. The following year came a new 7,456 cc (455 ci) V8, the largest engine ever to be dropped into a pony car.

This, though, was the era of increasing legislation for auto makers. As the decade progressed, power came down to meet emissions laws. Impact-resistant fibreglass bumpers were adopted for 1974, although to Pontiac's credit, the new 'droop snoot' actually did much to enhance the masculine looks of the Trans Am.

By now, the Trans Am had few rivals, much of its original competition having fallen by the wayside. Pontiac pushed on with the same basic shape until 1982, when a sleeker model with retractable headlamps superseded the classic design.

Pontiac Trans Am

Top speed:	201 km/h (125 mph)
0-96 km/h (0-60mph):	5.1 secs
Engine type:	V8
Displacement:	7,456 cc (455 ci)
Max power:	261 kW (350 bhp) @ 4,000 rpm
Max torque:	488 Nm (360 lb ft) @ 3,300 rpm
Weight:	1,596 kg (3,511 lb)
Economy:	3.2 km/l (9 mpg)
Transmission:	TH400 three-speed automatic
Brakes:	Four-wheel vented discs
Body/chassis:	Steel unitary chassis with steel body panels

UNITED STATES

257

Porsche 356

The 356 was the car that started the Porsche marque, gradually evolving from a raw VW Beetle-based special into a civilized and stylish sports tourer.

Swing axle rear suspension owes its origins to the Volkswagen, but was reworked. Nevertheless, the handling of the 356 could be tricky in the hands of an inexperienced driver.

Engines came in a variety of sizes throughout production, all based on the original Volkswagen Beetle air-cooled flat-four. The first engines developed little more than 30 kW (40 bhp), but by the end of production, the Carrera quad overhead camshaft unit had pushed the output up to 97 kW (130 bhp).

Drum brakes were used on all 356s up until 1963, when disc brakes made an appearance on the 356C.

Up until 1952, front windscreens were two piece items.

The lines of the 356 were clearly Volkswagen Beetle-based. But they would also define the essential Porsche look for decades to come. Even today, hints of the 356 can still be glimpsed in current models. Standard 356s came in coupé, cabriolet and speedster versions. This particular car is something special though, a Karmann Hardtop built for just one year. In essence, it is a cabriolet with a metal roof welded on.

GERMANY

The name of Porsche was already well known and respected in motoring circles by the time it became a household word in the 1950s. The Austrian Dr Ferdinand Porsche had been involved with vehicles and racing since the turn of the 20th century, most notably with the Volkswagen Beetle.

But it was his son, Ferry, who would bring the family name to the attention of the world. After the war, he decided that the small Porsche consultancy should build a Volkswagen-based sports special. The Beetle was chosen not just because of his father's involvement, but because it was the only car readily available in Austria at the time.

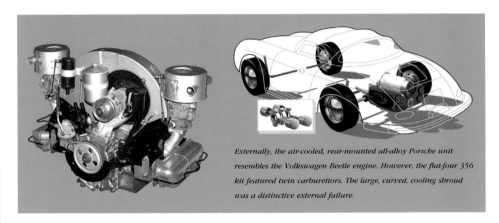

Externally, the air-cooled, rear-mounted all-alloy Porsche unit resembles the Volkswagen Beetle engine. However, the flat-four 356 kit featured twin carburettors. The large, curved, cooling shroud was a distinctive external failure.

The prototype Porsche 356 slipped quietly into the world in July 1947, production starting the following year. Although heavily VW-based, including the puny engine, the streamlined shape was still good for up to 129 km/h (80 mph).

Porsche grows up

With Porsche's move to Stuttgart in the early 1950s, the 356 became steadily more refined. Engine size and sophistication improved as sales went up, especially in the US, and Porsche's image received a further boost when a 356 won its class at Le Mans.

A Cabriolet joined the line-up in 1951, and was followed by the fabulous looking Speedster in 1954. In 1955, the 356A revamped the look of the car, adding a curved windscreen and bigger wheels, plus the option of a bigger engine. The Carrera variant featured a race-bred engine.

More facelifts followed, with the 356B of 1959 (sloping bonnet, new bumpers and headlamps), while 1963's 356C was the definitive version, with four-wheel disc brakes among other new features.

Soon after, the 911 was launched, and a fresh chapter started in the motoring history books.

Porsche 356

Top speed:	166 km/h (103 mph)
0-96 km/h (0-60mph):	13.0 secs
Engine type:	Flat-four
Displacement:	1,582 cc (97 ci)
Max power:	56 kW (75 bhp) @ 5,000 rpm
Max torque:	115 Nm (85 lb ft) @ 3,700 rpm
Weight:	936 kg (2,059 lb)
Economy:	8.9 km/l (25 mpg)
Transmission:	Four-speed manual
Brakes:	Four-wheel hydraulic drums
Body/chassis:	Steel platform chassis with steel bodywork, coupé or convertible

GERMANY

Porsche 911 Turbo

The Porsche 911 Turbo combined luxury motoring with turbocharged performance, wrapping it all up in one of the auto world's most evocative and widely-recognized shapes.

The rear-mounted engine was Porsche's usual all-alloy, overhead camshaft flat-six 'boxer'. The first Turbos had a three-litre (183 ci) engine, rising to 3.3 litres (201 ci) in 1977. Bosch K-Jetronic fuel injection was fitted, along with a single KKK turbocharger. Eventually, two smaller turbos would be used to eliminate turbo lag.

Brightwork was kept to a minimum on more modern 911s. This appearance was known as the 'black look'.

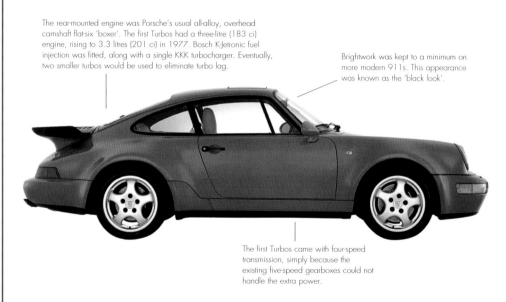

The first Turbos came with four-speed transmission, simply because the existing five-speed gearboxes could not handle the extra power.

The 911 shape is practically timeless. There are distinct echoes of the first Porsche, the 356, of 1948. The design has grown more muscular and less pure over the years, but the family relationship is clear, and distinctly Porsche.

The huge 'whale-tail' spoiler was a very noticeable feature. It provided downforce at high speeds, and also contained an intercooler, used to cool air entering the engine.

Flared wheel arches covered the fat tyres, which were of a different size at the front and rear on this 1991 example. The wheels made the steering very heavy, so power assistance was fitted.

GERMANY

263

I n a way, it is surprising that the original 911 concept survived as long as it did, let alone becoming such a legend. In a sports car world where new was always considered best and image was everything, the 911 steadfastly refused to change its traditional shape, remaining comfortably old-fashioned and notoriously tail-happy.

The 911 appeared in 1963 as a six-cylinder evolution of the 356. Power and specification got better as the years passed, but the most radical thing to happen to the car occurred in 1975, with the launch of the Turbo.

Porsche had been contemplating the Turbo for some time, with the aim of dominating the World Championship for

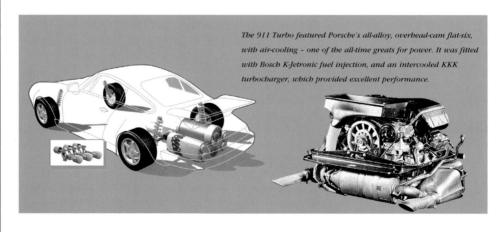

The 911 Turbo featured Porsche's all-alloy, overhead-cam flat-six, with air-cooling – one of the all-time greats for power. It was fitted with Bosch K-Jetronic fuel injection, and an intercooled KKK turbocharger, which provided excellent performance.

Manufacturers. Before it could do that though, it had sell 500 production examples to the public. There were serious doubts as to whether it would appeal.

Turbo take off

Despite costing almost twice the price of a normal 911, thanks to its well-appointed interior and extra gimmicks, the 911 Turbo took off immediately. Its seat-of-the-pants ride actually endeared it to drivers, who felt some sort of achievement at being able to 'tame' this difficult car. It could be genuinely terrifying, the fierce turbocharger suddenly cutting in when the car was already accelerating fast.

Porsche developed the Turbo over the next few decades, gradually improving the rear suspension. Engine size went up to 3.3 litres (201 ci) in 1977, and a five-speed gearbox belatedly appeared in 1988. By 1992, power output was up to 268 kW (360 bhp) on standard cars.

In 1995, the formula was changed when the 911 Turbo became four-wheel drive. The final air-cooled versions of the 911 were produced in 1997.

Porsche 911 Turbo

Top speed:	270 km/h (168 mph)
0-96 km/h (0-60mph):	4.9 secs
Engine type:	Flat-six
Displacement:	3,299 cc (201 ci)
Max power:	235 kW (315 bhp) @ 5,750 rpm
Max torque:	450 Nm (332 lb ft) @ 4,500 rpm
Weight:	1,488 kg (3,274 lb)
Economy:	4.4 km/l (12.4 mpg)
Transmission:	Five-speed manual
Brakes:	Four-wheel vented discs, 32.0 cm (12.6 in) at front, 29.7 cm (11.7 in) at rear
Body/chassis:	Steel monocoque with two-door coupé chassis

GERMANY

265

RANGE ROVER

The best 4 x 4 by far? The luxurious but tough Range Rover revolutionized off-roading in 1970, and remained a world-leader for the next 25 years.

The Range Rover towered above conventional cars. Even at its lowest point, clearance was 17.8 cm (7 in) and all the vulnerable parts which could be prone to damage from rocks were protected by the chassis frame.

Rover used its trusted and respected V8 engine to power the Range Rover, albeit slightly detuned to improve off-road qualities.

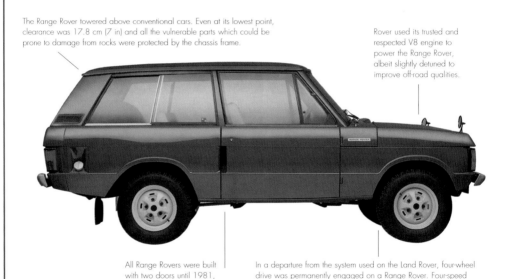

All Range Rovers were built with two doors until 1981, when a four-door version finally became available.

In a departure from the system used on the Land Rover, four-wheel drive was permanently engaged on a Range Rover. Four-speed transmission – with the option of overdrive – was the norm until 1983, when a five-speed gearbox was fitted.

In common with its less glamorous Land Rover sister, body panels on the Range Rover were aluminium, mounted on a tough steel chassis.

PVC trim and rubber floormats may not sound like the height of luxury, but compared to other off-roaders of the era, the Range Rover was lavishly equipped. However, the vehicle would gradually grow more opulent – and expensive – with leather, wood, air conditioning, air suspension and other options.

UNITED KINGDOM

267

It is difficult to imagine city and country streets and roads without a large variety of luxury off-roaders now. But prior to 1970, if you wanted to go cross-country, you had to accept austerity and harshness as part of the experience. And then came the Range Rover.

Designing an off-roader that came with frills was a big gamble for Rover. No other manufacturer had attempted to make anything like it before and it could have failed spectacularly in the marketplace. Instead, it would turn out to be one of motoring's landmarks.

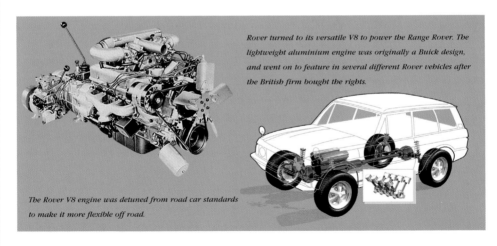

Rover turned to its versatile V8 to power the Range Rover. The lightweight aluminium engine was originally a Buick design, and went on to feature in several different Rover vehicles after the British firm bought the rights.

The Rover V8 engine was detuned from road car standards to make it more flexible off road.

The impetus came when Rover obtained a lightweight V8 engine from Buick. It was fitted to some of the firm's road cars, but was such a flexible unit that Rover started to look for alternative uses. With the leisure activity market taking off in the United States, the potential for a more refined version of the utility Land Rover was enormous.

A new, boxy body made of aluminium was designed with a large interior and a hatchback for versatility. The vehicle was extensively tested, from the frozen wastes of Norway to the baking Sahara desert before its launch in 1970.

Master at everything

It was a resounding success from the start. It was just as happy on the road as it was off, capable of going anywhere and tackling all environments with little fuss. But it was also refined enough to make it acceptable as an everyday vehicle, albeit an expensive one.

The simplistic but timeless elegance of the original design lasted for 25 years until replaced by an updated version in 1994.

Range Rover

Top speed:	159 km/h (99 mph)
0-96 km/h (0-60 mph):	12.9 secs
Engine type:	V8
Displacement:	3,528 cc (215 ci)
Max power:	97 kW (130 bhp) @ 5,000 rpm
Max torque:	278 Nm (205 lb ft) @ 3,000 rpm
Weight:	1,756 kg (3,864 lb)
Economy:	6 km/l (17 mpg)
Transmission:	Four-speed manual driving all four wheels
Brakes:	Four-wheel discs
Body/chassis:	Separate chassis with steel and aluminium two-door station wagon body

UNITED KINGDOM

269

ROLLS-ROYCE CAMARGUE

Rolls-Royces don't usually court controversy, but the Pininfarina-designed Camargue provoked heated debate. It also became the most expensive car of its era.

The design may be contentious, but the Camargue was the height of luxury inside. Apart from the established leather and wood, occupants also got split-level air conditioning, with the cooling capacity of 30 household refrigerators. The dashboard gauges were modelled on aircraft instruments.

Testing of the Camargue – initially codenamed the Delta – was done with a Bentley grille. But only one Bentley version would be built, a special order for a customer.

Whatever the opinion on the styling, the imposing road presence of the Camargue was undeniable. Few cars could dominate a highway in the same way.

Front fenders had small chrome 'tell-tales' at the corners, added to prevent expensive scrapes after testing revealed drivers had trouble telling the exact width of the car.

The Camargue was a heavy car, but some weight was saved by the doors, hood and trunklid being made out of aluminium. The rest of the body was steel.

Rolls-Royce's trademark grille was widened and shortened to fit the Camargue's front end. It was also angled slightly forward at the top, the only Rolls-Royce ever to feature this characteristic.

UNITED KINGDOM

271

When it was launched in 1975, the Camargue divided enthusiasts of the marque. Rolls-Royce's new and very costly flagship emerged with unconventional styling by the Italian Pininfarina design house. It would prove to be a major talking point.

The Camargue was the first time a non-British firm had been given a chance to design a production Rolls. Based on the Silver Shadow and using the same V8 engine, the result was a departure from the norm. Gone were the expected graceful curves and subtle proportions of past

The all-alloy V8 was standard fitting for all modern Rolls-Royces from 1959. It was given extra beef thanks to the use of different carburation, but Rolls-Royce never revealed just how much more power. It stayed in production into the 21st century, even after BMW took over the British firm.

creations, replaced by an enormous-looking vehicle with slab sides, sharp angles and an uncompromising frontal appearance thanks to its shortened and widened grille, which was also angled forwards. Tinkering with such an established tradition was considered heresy by many older enthusiasts, but was welcomed by others. Comparisons were drawn with Pininfarina's work on the Fiat 130 coupé and the Ferrari 365GT 2+2, which were considered too close for comfort.

The price of luxury

The Camargue's looks and sheer luxury guaranteed it attention, as did the price tag. Launch price was £29,500, making it the most expensive production car in the world. That could have bought two Silver Shadows. Within six years, it had almost tripled in price to £83,122. Small wonder that just 531 cars were sold in 10 years. A Camargue took six months to build, and at one stage, the waiting list was more than two years long.

Rolls-Royce has not attempted anything quite so radical since.

Rolls-Royce Camargue

Top speed:	209 km/h (130 mph)
0-96 km/h (0-60 mph):	9.7 secs
Engine type:	V8
Displacement:	6,750 cc (412 ci)
Max power:	164 kW (220 bhp) @ 4,000 rpm
Max torque:	447 Nm (330 lb ft) @ 2,500 rpm
Weight:	2,352 kg (5,175 lb)
Economy:	4.3 km/l (12 mpg)
Transmission:	Three-speed automatic
Brakes:	Vented discs at front, solid discs at rear
Body/chassis:	Unitary monocoque construction with subframes and steel two-door coupé body

UNITED KINGDOM

273

ROLLS-ROYCE SILVER CLOUD

The majestic and thoroughly traditional Silver Cloud is among the most elegant and refined of any Rolls-Royces to proudly carry the Spirit of Ecstasy mascot.

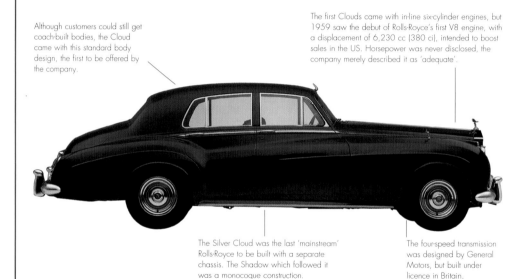

Although customers could still get coach-built bodies, the Cloud came with this standard body design, the first to be offered by the company.

The first Clouds came with in-line six-cylinder engines, but 1959 saw the debut of Rolls-Royce's first V8 engine, with a displacement of 6,230 cc (380 ci), intended to boost sales in the US. Horsepower was never disclosed, the company merely described it as 'adequate'.

The Silver Cloud was the last 'mainstream' Rolls-Royce to be built with a separate chassis. The Shadow which followed it was a monocoque construction.

The four-speed transmission was designed by General Motors, but built under licence in Britain.

Series I and II cars had single headlamps at the front. When the Cloud III came out in 1962, it had twin headlamps on either side, a look which would become something of a Rolls-Royce trademark.

Power steering and air conditioning were options from 1956.

The chrome bumpers were large items, and claimed by Rolls-Royce to have the thickest plating of any car available.

Every car came with a well-equipped toolkit in the rear, for those rare moments when a Ghost would 'fail to proceed'.

UNITED KINGDOM

275

U p until the Silver Cloud, all Rolls-Royces had their looks defined by the coachbuilders chosen to fit bodies onto the chassis the firm supplied. The Silver Cloud changed that, introducing standard bodywork for the first time.

Some might have seen that as a dilution of Rolls-Royce's exclusivity, but there's no denying that the Cloud's body was one of the most beautiful and aristocratic creations ever to grace four wheels. It was touted as 'the best car in the world', and anybody

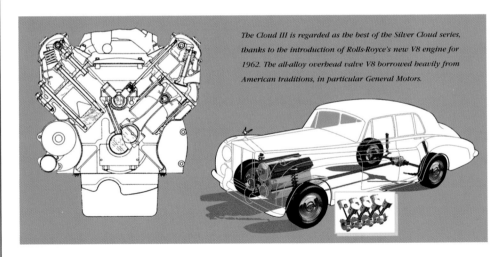

The Cloud III is regarded as the best of the Silver Cloud series, thanks to the introduction of Rolls-Royce's new V8 engine for 1962. The all-alloy overhead valve V8 borrowed heavily from American traditions, in particular General Motors.

seeing the grandiose exterior would be hard-pressed to disagree.

Intended as luxury transport for only the most privileged members of society, the interior was lined with the most expensive walnut, leather and carpeting available. It was a sanctuary of serenity; at 97 km/h (60 mph), the loudest noise you would hear would be the 'ticking of the clock', despite the large engine working under the hood.

The cars could also be bought as Bentleys, with only a different grille and badging distinguishing between the two marques.

Six to V8

When launched, Silver Clouds came with six-cylinder engines. However, mindful of sales in the all-important US market, a brand new, more powerful V8 engine was fitted in 1959. By then, power steering and air conditioning had already made the Cloud more refined.

The final major change came in 1962, with yet more power, a lower hood line and stylish but initially controversial twin-headlamp units.

Replacement for the classy Cloud came in 1965, with the Silver Shadow.

Rolls-Royce Silver Cloud (Silver Cloud II)

Top speed:	180 km/h (112 mph)
0-96 km/h (0-60 mph):	11.4 secs
Engine type:	V8
Displacement:	6,230 cc (380 ci)
Max power:	164 kW (220 bhp) @ 4,000 rpm
Max torque:	137 Nm (340 lb ft) @ 2,200 rpm
Weight:	2,072 kg (4,558 lb)
Economy:	4.3 km/l (12 mpg)
Transmission:	Four-speed automatic
Brakes:	Four-wheel drums
Body/chassis:	Separate chassis with steel four-door sedan body

UNITED KINGDOM

SAAB 99 TURBO

Saab took its competent but ordinary 99 sedan and transformed it into a cult street rocket, thanks to its pioneering and effective use of turbocharging.

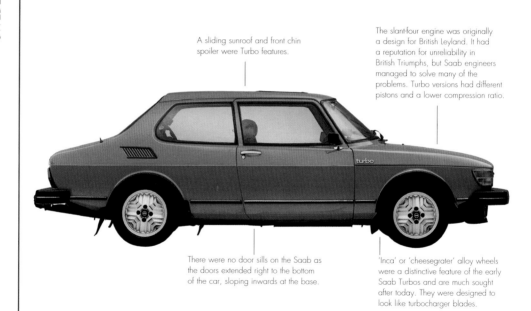

A sliding sunroof and front chin spoiler were Turbo features.

The slant-four engine was originally a design for British Leyland. It had a reputation for unreliability in British Triumphs, but Saab engineers managed to solve many of the problems. Turbo versions had different pistons and a lower compression ratio.

There were no door sills on the Saab as the doors extended right to the bottom of the car, sloping inwards at the base.

'Inca' or 'cheesegrater' alloy wheels were a distinctive feature of the early Saab Turbos and are much sought after today. They were designed to look like turbocharger blades.

Understated looks were part of the fun of owning a Saab 99 Turbo. It didn't look that much different from the standard version but performance was radically better and would embarrass many more expensive cars.

The three-door hatchback was the most common body style. Just 1,000 two-door Sedans – like this version – were made, making them extremely desirable today.

The hood had a novel opening arrangement. It slid forward and then hinged open at the front, improving access to the engine bay.

SWEDEN

In the mid-1970s, turbochargers on cars were still something of an oddity. They could be found on expensive and exotic sports vehicles but few ordinary people could contemplate owning such a luxury.

Then came the Saab 99 Turbo. The Swedish firm knew a thing or two about turbocharging and supercharging from its aviation and diesel truck work. But fears about performance, economy and emissions on its road cars made it look seriously at applying this technology to its 99 sedan.

The 99 range had been launched in 1967, and soon earned a reputation for

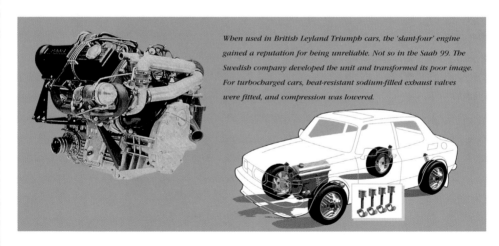

When used in British Leyland Triumph cars, the 'slant-four' engine gained a reputation for being unreliable. Not so in the Saab 99. The Swedish company developed the unit and transformed its poor image. For turbocharged cars, heat-resistant sodium-filled exhaust valves were fitted, and compression was lowered.

exceptional engineering and a robust, reliable character. However, 99s were never the most thrilling of cars, despite Saab's efforts to add a bit more excitement by adding fuel injection to some models.

Startling metamorphosis

So everybody was surprised by the 99's transformation from staid sedan into a real road burner in 1977. The small Swedish company had stolen the glory from all the major manufacturers by building the world's first turbocharged family sedan. The new car was affordable, but still capable of blistering performance, hitting 96 km/h (60 mph) in just 9.1 seconds, and not running out of steam until it was doing at least twice that speed – all from a relatively small-capacity engine.

What made this possible was the combination of a Bosch fuel injection system and a Garrett T3 turbocharger, together with heat-resistant sodium-filled exhaust valves. Except for a lowered compression ratio, much of the rest of the engine was standard.

In 1980, the 99 Turbo was replaced by the bigger 900 version.

Saab 99 Turbo

Top speed:	193 km/h (120 mph)
0-96 km/h (0-60 mph):	9.1 secs
Engine type:	In-line four
Displacement:	1,985 cc (121 ci)
Max power:	108 kW (145 bhp) @ 5,000 rpm
Max torque:	236 Nm (174 lb ft) @ 3,000 rpm
Weight:	1,234 kg (2,715 lb)
Economy:	7.8 km/l (22 mpg)
Transmission:	Four-speed manual
Brakes:	Four-wheel discs
Body/chassis:	Unitary construction steel monocoque two-door sedan or three-door hatchback body

SWEDEN

STUTZ BLACKHAWK

Few cars have been as flamboyantly outrageous as the hand-built Stutz Blackhawk, the revival of a great American name which took retro-styling to new levels.

The body was based on the Pontiac Grand Prix, but with modifications carried out in Italy. The Blackhawk pictured here was the two-door coupé version but also available was the Bearcat two-door convertible, the Victoria four-door sedan and the (over) stretched Royale and Diplomatica limousines.

Under the hood was Pontiac power in the form of a massive V8 with huge reserves of output and torque.

The styling was carried out by Virgil Exner of Chrysler fame and there were many of his distinctive trademarks on display in the design of the Blackhawk, such as the sweeping swathe line.

The 1930s-style side exhausts were purely for display. The real twin exhausts were concealed under the rear bumper.

Production costs were kept down thanks to the use of General Motors parts and the Pontiac Grand Prix chassis.

The spare tyre was not mounted on the trunk as it appeared. The lid had a novel cut-out, so it opened around the wheel.

Free-standing headlamps were another echo of automotive days gone by, although Virgil Exner also used them on his early 1960s Imperial range.

UNITED STATES

283

UNITED STATES

etro-styling is all the rage these days. Many manufacturers have tried to recapture past glories by blending classic cues with modern design. Most remain concept one-offs, but a few make it into mainstream production, usually to much acclaim.

However, none of these vehicles have managed to scale the grandiloquent heights of the car that first appeared almost 35 years ago, the Stutz Blackhawk. The Blackhawk was an ordinary Pontiac Grand Prix, transformed in Italy into something extraordinary for the rich, famous and extravagant.

The original Stutz Bearcat was known as one of the best sports cars of the early 20th century before it disappeared in the 1930s. In 1968, the marque name was revived

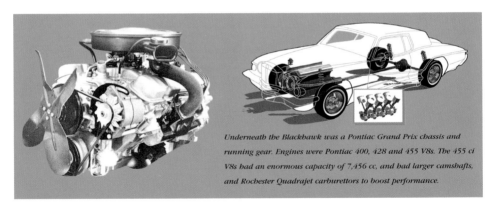

Underneath the Blackhawk was a Pontiac Grand Prix chassis and running gear. Engines were Pontiac 400, 428 and 455 V8s. The 455 ci V8s had an enormous capacity of 7,456 cc, and had larger camshafts, and Rochester Quadrajet carburettors to boost performance.

by New York investment banker James D O' Donnell and veteran Chrysler designer Virgil M. Exner, with backing from John DeLorean of Pontiac.

Revival of the fittest

Exner and O' Donnell started with a Pontiac Grand Prix and modified the design to the point where it was almost unrecognizable. Some of the alterations – such as the side exhausts, prominent radiator grille, separate headlamps and overdose of chromework – were considered garish, but the Blackhawk captured the luxury car mood of the time, thanks to its excessive looks and powerful V8 engine. Elvis Presley bought the first one off the production line in 1970, and other notable owners included Dean Martin, Frank Sinatra, Liberace, Lucille Ball and Muhammed Ali.

A lot of effort went into manufacturing the hand-built Stutz. The cars were built in Turin and Modena in Italy, before being shipped to New York and distributed by a Los Angeles agent.

Around 600 of these idiosyncratic vehicles were built before production ceased in around 1995.

Stutz Blackhawk

Top speed:	209 km/h (130 mph)
0-96 km/h (0-60mph):	9.4 secs
Engine type:	V8
Displacement:	7,456 cc (455 ci)
Max power:	238 kW (320 bhp) @ 4,400 rpm
Max torque:	569 Nm (420 lb ft) @ 3,200 rpm
Weight:	1,827 kg (4,021 lb)
Economy:	2.8 km/l (8 mpg)
Transmission:	GM TurboHydramatic 400 three-speed automatic
Brakes:	Discs at front, drums at rear
Body/chassis:	Separate steel chassis with hand-built coupé body

UNITED STATES

285

SUBARU IMPREZA TURBO

A master on the rally track, a master on the road. The handsome Subaru Impreza Turbo offers tremendous performance yet is reasonably priced and reliable.

The Turbo's lines are discreet, although the front air dam, fog lights, rear spoiler and hood intakes for the intercooler hint at its true potential.

Flat-four engines are rare in modern cars, although air-cooled versions have previously appeared in the Volkswagen Beetle and Porsche 356. However, the Impreza's 'boxer' engine is vastly different to those simplistic units. It bristles with high technology, including multipoint fuel injection, a high compression ratio and an intercooled Hitachi turbocharger. It is capable of kicking out 155 kW (208 bhp).

The ratios in the five-speed gearbox are grouped closely together. That puts the emphasis on acceleration, resulting in a car that can outgun many more expensive sports cars.

Subaru has always been at the forefront of four-wheel drive, and its appearance on the Turbo gave the Impreza magnetic road holding and enhanced safety in poor driving conditions.

A car with such intense performance needs to be able to stop quickly as well. The Turbo comes with big vented disc brakes at the front and even larger solid ones at the rear. Anti-lock braking is fitted as standard.

JAPAN

287

JAPAN

According to the old adage, competition improves the breed. In the case of Subaru, it improved the company as well, making it very successful and famous. Prior to the Impreza, the Japanese manufacturer built competent, but ultimately dull and ordinary vehicles, albeit ones with all-wheel drive.

It needed something special to change Subaru's dowdy image. It needed something like the Impreza.

Based on the Legacy chassis, and using the same 122 ci (two-litre) flat-four engine, the new Impreza of 1992 was far more dynamic than its bigger sibling. In Turbo trim, it was little short of mind-blowing.

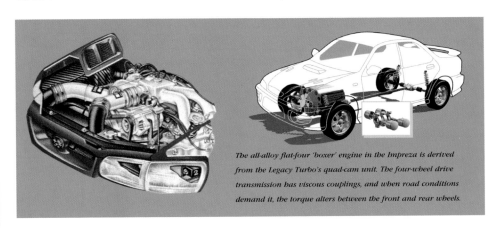

The all-alloy flat-four 'boxer' engine in the Impreza is derived from the Legacy Turbo's quad-cam unit. The four-wheel drive transmission has viscous couplings, and when road conditions demand it, the torque alters between the front and rear wheels.

Wolf in sheep's clothing

The Impreza didn't look much. It was neat enough but the styling was anonymous. However, all it took was a turn of a key and an open road to see just how special it was. Acceleration was astonishing, yet the Impreza clung tenaciously to any surface in any weather conditions, thanks to its four driven wheels. Corners could be tackled at the kinds of speeds which would leave lesser cars in serious trouble. Yet its price was much less than the majority of its rivals.

The first rally success came in 1994. After that, it just didn't stop. There was the World Championship in 1995, while the Subaru team scooped the Constructors title in 1995, 1996 and 1997. The blue and gold-liveried competition cars became synonymous with rally victory.

The Impreza Turbo remains in production today, and it's still winning major rallies. There have been changes, both to the engine and the styling, although the bug-eyed look for the beginning of the 21st century was not well received. But the original spirit remains, making the Impreza still one of the best road cars available today.

Subaru Impreza Turbo

Top speed:	230 km/h (143 mph)
0-96 km/h (0-60mph):	6.4 secs
Engine type:	Flat-four
Displacement:	1,994 cc (122 ci)
Max power:	155 kW (208 bhp) @ 5,600 rpm
Max torque:	290 Nm (214 lb ft) @ 4,000 rpm
Weight:	1,309 kg (2,879 lb)
Economy:	10.3 km/l (29 mpg)
Transmission:	Five-speed manual
Brakes:	Vented discs, 22.9 cm (9 in) diameter at front, solid discs, 23.1 cm (9.1 in) diameter at rear
Body/chassis:	Integral chassis with four-door sedan body

JAPAN

Toyota MR2

The name means 'Midships Recreational Two-seater', hardly a catchy name for the Japanese car that revitalized the concept of the affordable mid-engined sports car.

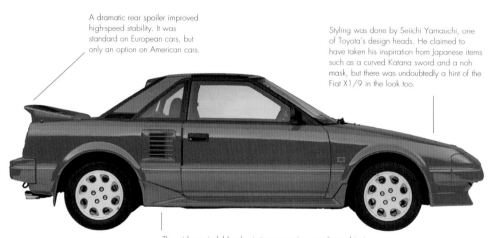

A dramatic rear spoiler improved high-speed stability. It was standard on European cars, but only an option on American cars.

Styling was done by Seiichi Yamauchi, one of Toyota's design heads. He claimed to have taken his inspiration from Japanese items such as a curved Katana sword and a noh mask, but there was undoubtedly a hint of the Fiat X1/9 in the look too.

The mid-mounted 16-valve twin-cam engine wasn't very big in terms of displacement, but it didn't need to be with the compact, lightweight MR2. The engine was capable of revving from idle to the redline in less than a second. And being Japanese, it was tough and reliable too. A supercharged version arrived in 1986, which endowed the MR2 with almost supercar performance.

Pop-up headlamps were driven by electrical motors, and helped retain the smooth look when down.

The Targa style roof – the 'T-Bar' in Toyota parlance – was introduced to all markets by 1987, and made the MR2 into (almost) a convertible.

Disc brakes were fitted all round, although only the front ones were vented.

JAPAN

Japanese cars started their assault on European and American markets from the 1970s onwards. Far East manufacturers took time to study and absorb what other auto makers were doing and then improved on it. Although rarely original, products from Japan were often much better than the cars they aspired to emulate.

Such was the case with the Toyota MR2. Mid-engined sports cars had long been the preserve of exotic manufacturers like Ferrari, Lamborghini and Maserati, but few firms had managed to produce affordable versions for the mass-market. One which did was Fiat, with the X1/9, in production from 1972 to 1989. It was a clever package with few rivals ... at least until the MR2 arrived.

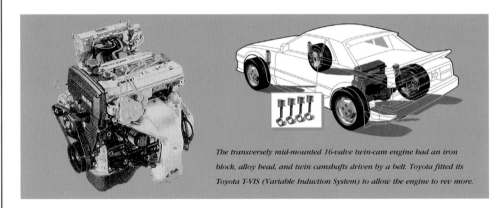

The transversely mid-mounted 16-valve twin-cam engine had an iron block, alloy head, and twin camshafts driven by a belt. Toyota fitted its Toyota T-VIS (Variable Induction System) to allow the engine to rev more.

The MR2 was born as the SV-3 mid-engined concept car at the 1983 Tokyo Motor Show. It proved such a popular attraction that it was put into production a year later, and launched to the rest of the world in 1985.

Origami theme

Styling followed the Japanese 'origami' look of sharp, almost severe, angular lines and a wedge-shaped appearance. Many of the features of the X1/9 were either repeated or subtly improved in the Japanese wannabe, giving the car great handling, with a 45/55 front/rear balance.

Sales – particularly in the US – were brisk, especially by 1986 when a supercharged version was launched. Open-topped motoring also became possible, thanks to the Targa roof model, known as the T-Bar.

The original MR2 managed to sell just over 166,000 units by the time it was superseded by the more curvaceous, larger second series in 1991. The third generation MR2 is still in production today and is very popular throughout the world.

Toyota MR2

Top speed:	195 km/h (121 mph)
0-96 km/h (0-60mph):	8.4 secs
Engine type:	In-line four
Displacement:	1,587 cc (97 ci)
Max power:	84 kW (112 bhp) @ 6,600 rpm
Max torque:	131 Nm (97 lb ft) @ 4,800 rpm
Weight:	1,086 kg (2,390 lb)
Economy:	8.1 km/l (23 mpg)
Transmission:	Five-speed manual
Brakes:	Vented discs, 24.4 cm (9.6 in) diameter at front, solid discs, 24.4 cm (9.6 in) diameter at rear
Body/chassis:	Unitary monocoque construction with steel two-door, two-seater body

JAPAN

TRIUMPH TR4

The Triumph TR4 continued the traditional British sports car theme established by the TR2 and TR3, but added sharp modern Italian styling by Giovanni Michelotti.

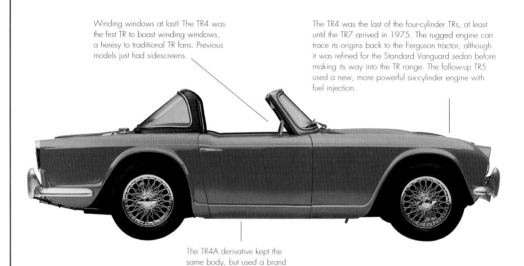

Winding windows at last! The TR4 was the first TR to boast winding windows, a heresy to traditional TR fans. Previous models just had sidescreens.

The TR4 was the last of the four-cylinder TRs, at least until the TR7 arrived in 1975. The rugged engine can trace its origins back to the Ferguson tractor, although it was refined for the Standard Vanguard sedan before making its way into the TR range. The follow-up TR5 used a new, more powerful six-cylinder engine with fuel injection.

The TR4A derivative kept the same body, but used a brand new chassis with all-independent suspension underneath.

Although the TR4's body design was completely new, there were some echoes of the previous cars at the front, with the shrouded circular headlamps reminiscent of the old bug-eye lights.

An attractive Surrey top was an alternative to the soft top, or the full metal hardtop.

The power bulge in the bonnet was needed to clear the tops of the twin SU carburettors. When the six-cylinder engine was fitted, Triumph kept this feature because it looked so good!

The British sports car market was very competitive by the turn of the 1960s. Triumph and MG in particular were fierce rivals, especially in the United States. While MG had updated its image with the MGA, Triumph had remained resolutely traditional, building old school sports cars.

Triumph's problem was that it didn't have a lot of money to spend. Italian stylist Giovanni Michelotti was given the brief to start work on a thoroughly modern-looking design, using the TR3 chassis and running gear to reduce costs. After several false starts he came up with an attractive and definitive body shape.

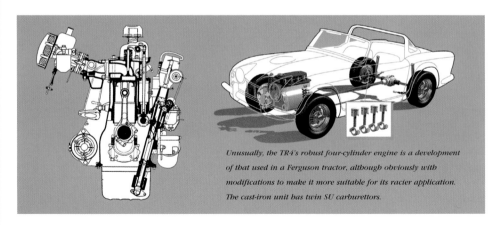

Unusually, the TR4's robust four-cylinder engine is a development of that used in a Ferguson tractor, although obviously with modifications to make it more suitable for its racier application. The cast-iron unit has twin SU carburettors.

Launched in 1961, the TR4 looked very different to previous Triumphs, the crisp lines just right for the new decade. It was more comfortable, practical and spacious than many of its contemporaries. Although much of the TR3 remained underneath, it was updated, with rack-and-pinion steering and servo brakes appearing. A larger 2,138 cc (130 ci) engine was made an option.

Adding an A

Sales were good, certainly strong enough to worry Triumph's rivals. The TR4 remained largely untouched until 1965, when it evolved into the TR4A. This time, the body stayed the same but the underpinnings got a makeover. All-independent suspension was fitted, a move which improved handling, although US dealers demanded that a version with the old live beam axle be made available too, as a cut-price alternative.

The next big move for the TR model came in 1967, with the appearance of a six-cylinder engine and fuel injection, although the latter was not available in the US.

The TR4 was significant for turning Triumph into a modern, viable alternative to MG and Austin-Healey.

Triumph TR4

Top speed:	177 km/h (110 mph)
0-96 km/h (0-60mph):	10.7 secs
Engine type:	In-line four
Displacement:	2,138 cc (130 ci)
Max power:	75 kW (100 bhp) @ 4,600 rpm
Max torque:	173 Nm (128 lb ft) @ 3,350 rpm
Weight:	1,000 kg (2,200 lb)
Economy:	9.9 km/l (28 mpg)
Transmission:	Four-speed manual with optional triple overdrive
Brakes:	Discs at front, drums at rear
Body/chassis:	Separate chassis with steel two-door roadster body

UNITED KINGDOM

Volkswagen Beetle

Volkswagen's ubiquitous Beetle is probably the world's favourite classic. Over 60 years after it first appeared, it is still being made to the original concept.

Even the most modern Beetle engine is still heavily related to the 19 kW (25 bhp) pre-war design of Austrian Franz Xavier Reimspiess. The flat-four air-cooled engine is made of aluminium and rear-mounted. Among its many attributes is the fact that it can easily be removed.

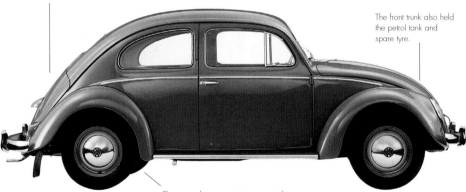

The front trunk also held the petrol tank and spare tyre.

The torsion-bar suspension was used all the way up to the 1970s, when the Super Beetle became available with MacPherson struts up front, and disc brakes on the leading wheels.

Fenders were bolt-on, for ease of repair in an accident. Even the body could be taken off the chassis just by undoing a few bolts. It all added up to a modifier's dream, and old Beetles have often formed the basis for custom cars.

The rear window gradually got larger with the passing years. The original design had no back window at all, but a split rear window was added when the car went into production. Then came an oval design, and finally a rectangular window, which has lasted until the present day.

It is ageless, classless and timeless. Everybody loves the ugly Bug, with its friendly, geeky looks and big personality. Disney even made movies about the adorable little car.

The truth, initially at least, was somewhat different. The mastermind behind the Beetle was Adolf Hitler. His plan was to create a car accessible to everyone – hence Volkswagen (literally, 'people's car') – and he brought in Dr Ferdinand Porsche to make it happen.

The war disrupted plans (although some Beetle-based vehicles did fight) and the car would have died amid the wreckage of the

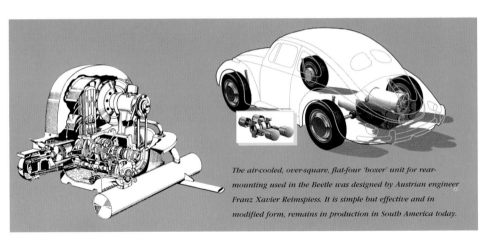

The air-cooled, over-square, flat-four 'boxer' unit for rear-mounting used in the Beetle was designed by Austrian engineer Franz Xavier Reimspiess. It is simple but effective and in modified form, remains in production in South America today.

defeated Germany had the British Army not taken over the Wolfsburg factory where it was made. In 1948, control was handed back to Germany, and home sales picked up.

World car

Under the general management of Heinz Nordhoff, the Beetle became a global phenomenon. He recognized that the future lay in exports, and worked tirelessly to get his funny little car accepted in foreign markets. The first US spec model came in 1949, and sales to North America grew every year after that, backed by some of the most creative and entertaining marketing campaigns ever. By the 1960s, it seemed like every other vehicle in America was a Bug, and the rugged and reliable VW had taken over most other countries as well.

Improvements were made every year, but by the 1970s, the Beetle was outdated. In 1978, production stopped in Germany, but continued in Latin America until 2003. The enduring success of the Beetle prompted VW to release a modern tribute in 1998. But there is still nothing like the original.

Volkswagen Beetle (1970 1300 model)	
Top speed:	125 km/h (78 mph)
0-96 km/h (0-60 mph):	16.1 secs
Engine type:	Flat-four
Displacement:	1,285 cc (78 ci)
Max power:	33 kW (44 bhp) @ 4,100 rpm
Max torque:	110 Nm (81 lb ft) @ 2,600 rpm
Weight:	761 kg (1,675 lb)
Economy:	8.1 km/l (23 mpg)
Transmission:	Four-speed manual
Brakes:	Four-wheel drums, 22.9 cm (9 in) diameter
Body/chassis:	Separate steel body on pressed steel backbone and floor platform chassis

GERMANY

VOLKSWAGEN GOLF GTI

Volkswagen invented a whole new concept with the inspired Golf GTi – the 'hot hatch'. Its runaway success spawned a legion of imitators from rival manufacturers.

The neat, compact shape of the Golf was the work of Italian stylist Giorgetto Giugiaro. Modern Golfs still have similar lines, although they are larger cars.

The front-wheel drive GTi handled superbly, thanks to its Bilstein shock absorbers and both front and rear anti-roll bars. The suspension was also lower and firmer.

The GTi didn't look that different from the standard model, but flared wheel arches and alloy wheels hinted at extra performance. The wider arches weren't just for display though – they were necessary for the bigger tyres.

Front vented disc brakes were more than adequate for halting the GTi. The rear ones were drums.

The blunt front didn't help aerodynamics, but a front spoiler fitted to the GTi was one way of improving the air flow.

The opening rear on the GTi spawned the term 'hot hatch' to describe it.

Bosch fuel injection meant smoother power delivery and more horsepower.

The sedan body would eventually be joined by a popular convertible version. The cabriolet was 12 per cent heavier to make the shell stiffer.

GERMANY

A ll car companies dream of creating a legend, a car that goes down in automotive history as a world-class product. In the case of Volkswagen, it managed to come up with two such motoring icons.

The first was the Beetle. And it would be the Bug that, indirectly, lead to the second of VW's great achievements, the Golf, and in particular, the performance GTi version.

VW had made several attempts to develop a Beetle successor, but with little success.

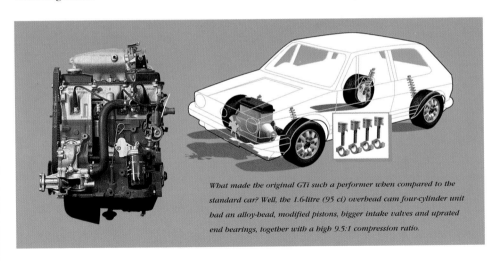

What made the original GTi such a performer when compared to the standard car? Well, the 1.6-litre (95 ci) overhead cam four-cylinder unit had an alloy-head, modified pistons, bigger intake valves and uprated end bearings, together with a high 9.5:1 compression ratio.

The Golf of 1974 was a panic move, an all-or-nothing effort to finally replace a popular but aging anachronism. It succeeded better than VW expected.

Behind the scenes though, engineers were secretly working on something a bit more special. The suspension was stiffened up and Bosch fuel injection was used to boost horsepower and performance. But there was little enthusiasm from VW management, who saw a only a potential market of 5,000 customers.

They turned out to be totally wrong. The Golf GTi became the Mini Cooper of the 1970s, winning many friends with its combination of sportiness and practicality, all wrapped up in the typical package of German reliability.

Soon, other manufacturers would be rushing to capitalize on the whole new 'hot hatch' market created by the GTi, but few were able to touch the original for sheer fun and usability.

Subsequent versions of the GTi became fatter and slower, leaving the Mk I to become a cult classic.

Volkswagen Golf GTi (1976 1600 model)

Top speed:	172 km/h (107 mph)
0-96 km/h (0-60 mph):	9.8 secs
Engine type:	In-line four
Displacement:	1,558 cc (95 ci)
Max power:	82 kW (110 bhp) @ 6,100 rpm
Max torque:	135 Nm (100 lb ft) @ 5,000 rpm
Weight:	865 kg (1,904 lb)
Economy:	5.7 km/l (16 mpg)
Transmission:	Five-speed manual
Brakes:	Vented discs, 24.1 cm (9.5 in) diameter at front, drums, 17.8 cm (7 in) diameter at rear
Body/chassis:	Steel monocoque with two-door, four-seat hatchback body

GERMANY

VOLVO P1800

Volvo's reputation was based on building safe, solid and sober cars. The P1800 was its first major successful attempt to break this image.

A sports sedan it may have been, but typical Volvo practicality was part of the design. The big trunk, flanked by chrome-tipped rounded fins, could hold lots of luggage.

The first cars had a 1,780 cc (109 ci) engine, which grew to two litres (121 ci) at the end of the 1960s. In 1970, even more power was added by fuel injection. With this technology, the final cars could boast a power output of 96 kW (130 bhp).

The charismatic styling was the work of a Swedish boat designer, Pelle Petterson, although it was refined by the Italian styling house, Frua.

The four-speed all-synchromesh gearbox had overdrive from 1963.

The distinctive split front bumper and egg-crate grille indicates that this car was built in Britain, by Jensen. After quality control problems, production was shifted back to Sweden.

It's a Volvo, so ruggedness came as standard. High quality, galvanized steel was used in the body, while the floorpan was extensively undersealed. As is usual with Volvos, a P1800 would long outlast its rivals, something the company made great use of in its advertising.

B efore Roger Moore slipped on James Bond's dinner suit and made the Lotus Esprit famous, he helped turn the Volvo P1800 into a star as well. As Simon Templar – the Saint – Moore drove one of the flamboyant Volvos, after Jaguar refused to lend the producers of the show an E-type. Bad news for Jaguar, good news for Volvo, because it made the Swedish sports sedan immortal.

Volvo had tried unsuccessfully to break into the sports market on a number of occasions. Its image as a manufacturer of dull but worthy cars remained. It cracked

The P1800 marked the debut of Volvo's new, sturdy B18 five-bearing crankshaft engine, fitted with a single camshaft. To inject some sportiness into this otherwise mundane four-cylinder motor, it had twin SU carburettors attached, and an oil cooler was fitted as standard.

it with the P1800 though, a fast two-seater with striking styling, the result of efforts by novice designer Pelle Petterson, and the Italian design company, Frua. The engine was a development of the unit already proven in the Volvo Amazon and was tough, dependable and had a great reputation.

Back to Sweden

The P1800 was first shown in 1960, with production starting the following year. Due to lack of space at its Swedish plants, production of the P1800 was entrusted to Jensen in Britain. However, Jensen soon found out that it had taken on more than it could manage and quality problems became rife. So, in 1963, Volvo ended the contract and started production back in Gothenburg. The car was renamed the 1800S, to denote it was now being manufactured in Sweden.

More a grand tourer than a serious sports car, the 1800S sold well, but not spectacularly. Power was increased in 1969 and, in 1970,

performance was much improved by the addition of fuel injection, with the 1800E.

The dated-looking Volvo was dropped in 1972, although a short-lived sporting station wagon, the1800ES, continued until 1973.

Volvo P1800

Top speed:	169 km/h (105 mph)
0-96 km/h (0-60 mph):	14.0 secs
Engine type:	In-line four
Displacement:	1,780 cc (109 ci)
Max power:	75 kW (100 bhp) @ 5,500 rpm
Max torque:	146 Nm (108 lb ft) @ 4,000 rpm
Weight:	1,092 kg (2,404 lb)
Economy:	7.3 km/l (20.5 mpg)
Transmission:	Four-speed manual with optional overdrive
Brakes:	Discs at front, drums at rear
Body/chassis:	Steel monocoque with two-door coupé body

SWEDEN

WILLYS JEEP

Glamour does not enter the equation with the Willys Jeep. It was a wartime mule, built for battle, but eventually turning into an unlikely motoring star.

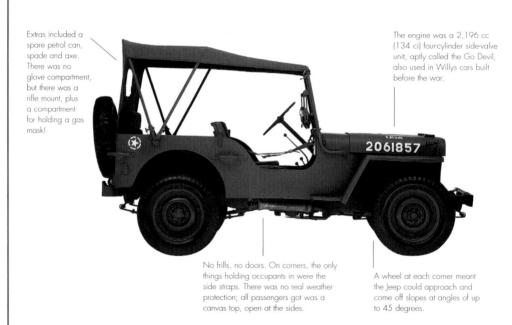

Extras included a spare petrol can, spade and axe. There was no glove compartment, but there was a rifle mount, plus a compartment for holding a gas mask!

The engine was a 2,196 cc (134 ci) four-cylinder side-valve unit, aptly called the Go Devil, also used in Willys cars built before the war.

No frills, no doors. On corners, the only things holding occupants in were the side straps. There was no real weather protection; all passengers got was a canvas top, open at the sides.

A wheel at each corner meant the Jeep could approach and come off slopes at angles of up to 45 degrees.

Bodywork was simple so it could be repaired easily, vital considering the sort of treatment Jeeps got from drivers ... and enemy forces!

Springs were stiffer on the left-hand side to cope with engine weight.

The gearbox was only three-speed, but for off-road use, there was a two-speed transfer case. The driver could also select all-wheel or just rear-wheel drive.

The box-section chassis had flexibility built in, so the frame could twist on rough terrain.

UNITED STATES

In 1940, the US Government released its 'Rearmament Program' to vehicle manufacturers. One of its requirements was for a 'Truck, 4 x 4, Light' – the somewhat less catchy title for the vehicle which would go on to become the Jeep.

135 companies were asked to build a prototype within 49 days. It was such a daunting task that only three firms responded, American Bantam, Willys Overland and Ford. All received contracts, but in 1941, design was standardized on

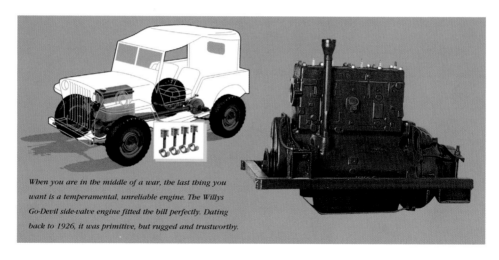

When you are in the middle of a war, the last thing you want is a temperamental, unreliable engine. The Willys Go-Devil side-valve engine fitted the bill perfectly. Dating back to 1926, it was primitive, but rugged and trustworthy.

a combination of the best features of the three vehicles.

GPW becomes Jeep

The new GPW (as Ford called it) soon earned the nickname Jeep, either because of its military designation, or after Eugene the Jeep from the Popeye cartoon. Whatever the origin, the GPW and the GI were ideal together, the Jeep becoming the modern equivalent of the cavalry horse.

According to General Dwight D. Eisenhower, the three tools that won the war in Europe were the Dakota plane, the landing craft and the Jeep. The Jeep was incredibly versatile, mobilizing Allied forces throughout the world, and making an incalculable contribution to the war effort. 650,000 were built during hostilities. It was its sheer simplicity that made it practically unstoppable and there was so little to go wrong that usually, only enemy action could halt it.

The Jeep name continued after the war, thanks to Willys trademarking it. It has continued on 4 x 4 vehicles, both military and civilian, ever since, despite takeovers of the original manufacturer by corporations such as AMC and Chrysler.

Willys Jeep

Top speed:	100 km/h (62 mph)
0-96 km/h:	
(0-60 mph):	30 secs
Engine type:	In-line four
Displacement:	2,196 cc (134 ci)
Max power:	45 kW (60 bhp) @ 3,600 rpm
Max torque:	142 Nm (105 lb ft) @ 2,000 rpm
Weight:	1,115 kg (2,453 lb)
Economy:	4.9 km/l (13.8 mpg)
Transmission:	Three-speed manual
Brakes:	Four-wheel drums
Body/chassis:	Steel frame with doorless open steel body

UNITED STATES

INDEX

INDEX